The Sky Warriors

The Sky Warriors

Operation Sindoor Unveiled

Vishnu Som

JUGGERNAUT BOOKS
C-I-128, First Floor, Sangam Vihar, Near Holi Chowk,
New Delhi 110080, India

First published by Juggernaut Books 2026

10 9 8 7 6 5 4 3 2

P-ISBN: 9789353455767
E-ISBN: 9789353459567

Typeset in Adobe Caslon Pro by R. Ajith Kumar, Noida

Printed at Saurabh Printers Pvt. Ltd.

This book is dedicated to my wife, Arundhati — the rock star in my life who holds together our family and everything that matters to us. A brilliant editor and author herself, she has been a constant source of encouragement, telling me often that it's time to get on to writing a book. Well, here it is!

And to my boys, Ishayu and Ahan, for always being there for me. There is nothing more important to me than the love of my family.

Contents

Contents

List of Characters

Many people were interviewed for this book. Here is a list of the key subjects whose stories and voices are featured.

The Commanders

- Air Chief Marshal A.P. Singh: Chief of the Air Staff
- Air Marshal Narmdeshwar Tiwari: Vice Chief of the Indian Air Force (IAF)
- Air Marshal A.K. Bharti: Director General of Air Operations
- Air Marshal P.K. Vohra: Senior Air Staff Officer (SASO) of the Western Air Command

The Pilots

- Group Captain Manav Bhatia: Commanding Officer of a Sukhoi-30 MKI squadron

- Group Captain Ranjeet Singh Sidhu: Commanding Officer of a Rafale squadron, awarded the Vir Chakra
- Group Captain Kunal Kalra: Flight Commander of a Sukhoi-30 MKI squadron, awarded the Vir Chakra.

The Men on the Ground

- Group Captain Animesh Patni: S-400 Unit Commanding Officer, AF Station Adampur, awarded the Vir Chakra
- Group Captain A.G. Kumar*: Chief Operations Officer, AF Station Adampur
- Group Captain Sunil Gupta*: Commanding Officer of an Akash missile unit deployed near the Line of Control
- Group Captain Jijo Jose Ovelil: Chief Operations Officer, AF Station Srinagar
- Commander of an Integrated Air Command and Control System (IACCS) node that covers North India

---

*To protect the privacy and anonymity of the individual involved, name and some identifying details have been changed or omitted.

Timeline[1]

- 22 April 2025: Pahalgam attack
- 23 April 2025: High-level meeting to plan military options
- 24 April 2025: Military options presented, planning for operations continues
- 5 May 2025: Date and time for Operation Sindoor finalised

7 May 2025 (early morning): India launches Operation Sindoor

- 1.05 a.m.: India hits nine terror targets in Pakistan and Pakistan-occupied Kashmir.
- 1.05–2.00 a.m.: Intense Indo-Pak air battle, Pakistan claims hits on multiple IAF fighter aircraft

- S-400 surface-to-air missile unit in Adampur shoots down a PAF JF-17 fighter.[*]

7 May (night)–8 May 2025: Pakistan's aggression

- Multiple Pakistani missile and drone attack attempts on 15 Indian military bases.[2]
- Pakistan violates Indian airspace with 300 drones and loiter munitions ('kamikaze' drones).
- Pakistan fires CM-400 cruise missiles.

7 May (night)–8 May 2025: India responds

- India's integrated counter Unmanned Aerial Systems (UAS) grid responds to drone attacks.
- Indian Armed Forces target Pakistan air defence radars at multiple locations.[3]
- Pakistani air defence system in Lahore neutralised in Indian strike.[4]

8 May (night)–9 May 2025: Pakistan's aggression

- Increased and indiscriminate pan-front drone activity by Pakistan at 36 locations.[5]

---

[*]An account of the IAF shootdown of a PAF JF-17 fighter on May 7 is detailed in this book.

- 300–400 Pakistani drones detected.
- Pakistan deploys loiter munitions, rockets and air-launched weapons.
- Attempts to saturate Indian air defence, localise and target radars, surface-to-air missile systems
- Pakistan attempts to target Indian Army (IA) and IAF assets and locations.
- Pakistan fires CM-400 cruise missiles.
- Pakistan attempts to target Indian military infrastructure, Indian radars and surface-to-air missile systems.
- Pakistan artillery launches heavy attacks along the Line of Control.

8 May (night)–9 May 2025: India strikes back

- Multiple Pakistani drones and loiter munitions intercepted by the Indian air defence systems
- IAF focusses on 'shaping operations' in case of further escalation.
- India launches armed drones at four Pakistani air defence sites, proof of the complete destruction of one location shared, others significantly damaged.[6]

9 May (night)–10 May 2025: Pakistan's aggression

- Intense pan-front drone activity at more than 26 locations.[7]
- Pakistan fires air-launched standoff weapons, drones, rockets, armed drones and loiter munitions.
- Attempted attacks directed on IAF Bases, IACCS assets and S-400 missile units
- Insignificant damage to a few IAF bases, some injuries reported to personnel at Udhampur.
- All projectiles intercepted or jammed and fall on vacant land.

9 May (night)–10 May 2025: India strikes back

- Indian integrated air defences intercept incoming Pakistani drones and missiles.
- Major Indian retaliation to the Pakistani escalation – at least 10 Pakistan bases/facilities targeted.
- Pakistan's airbases, sensors and surface-to-air missile systems targeted.
- 2.00–5.00 a.m.: Chaklala, Rahawali, Rafiqui, Rahim Yar Khan, Sukkur, Murid and Nayachor attacked with missiles.[8]

- 10.00 a.m.–12.00 p.m.: Sargodha, Bholari and Jacobabad attacked with missiles.
- IAF S-400 surface-to-air missile units engage multiple PAF fighters. IAF shoots down Pakistan's jets.
- IAF shoots down Pakistan's Airborne Early Warning & Control (AEW&C)/Electronic Intelligence aircraft.[*]
- Multiple PAF aircraft destroyed in hangars, runways cratered and Command and Control nodes hit.
- IAF on the offensive – primary PAF bases targeted at will.

10 May 2025: Ceasefire

- 3.35 p.m.: Pakistan's Director General of Military Operations (DGMO), Major General Kashif Abdullah, calls India's DGMO, Lieutenant General Rajiv Ghai to discuss a ceasefire.[9]
- 5.00 p.m.: Ceasefire takes effect officially. However, sporadic attacks from PAF continue for two days; the IAF respond in adequate measure.

---

[*]Detailed account of the IAF shootdown of a PAF Airborne Early Warning/Electronic Intelligence Aircraft is given in this book.

Map of India's Strikes

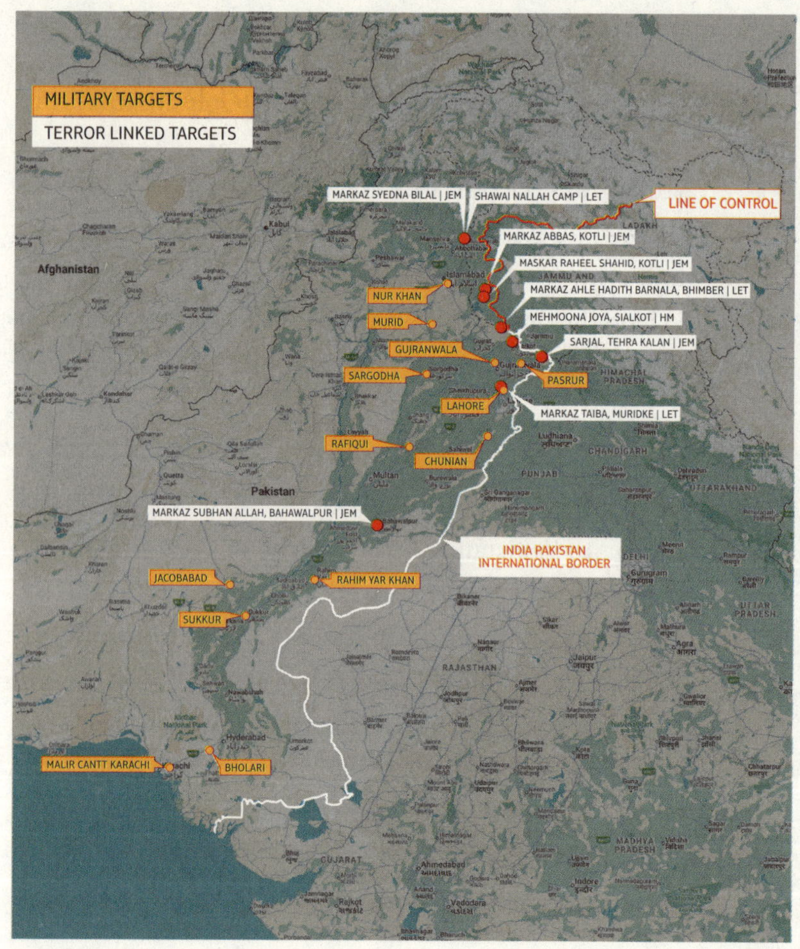

Introduction

On 22 April 2025, a gruesome terrorist attack shattered the peace of the country. Twenty-six civilians, mostly Hindu tourists, were killed by three armed militants who systematically identified and executed men after asking and methodically ascertaining that they were non-Muslims, in plain sight of their begging families, with the sole exception of a pony owner who protested.

Prime Minister Narendra Modi named India's military response to the Pahalgam terror attack Operation Sindoor: a name chosen to reflect the deep pain and resolve of a nation struck by one of the most gut-wrenching terror incidents on its soil.

In his address to the nation, he explained that in Indian tradition, sindoor – the red vermilion powder worn by married women in the parting of their hair – symbolises the sanctity of marriage and a husband's protection. By killing husbands in front of their wives, the terrorists had, in effect, wiped away that sindoor.

'Every terrorist must know the consequence of wiping the sindoor from the foreheads of our sisters and daughters,' he declared. The grief of those widows had transformed into national determination. In his words from Bikaner: 'Not blood, but sindoor flows in my veins – sindoor that turns into barood [gunpowder].'

Operation Sindoor became more than a code name. It carried the weight of cultural loss and the promise of justice. On 7 May, Indian forces struck terror camps in Pakistan, delivering what Prime Minister Narendra Modi described as a fitting response to those who had dared to desecrate something so sacred to millions of Indians. The four-day war that followed saw the most intense air battles India and Pakistan had waged since the 1971 war that had resulted in the liberation of Bangladesh.

On 31 July 1999, I strapped myself into the rear seat of a Mirage 2000 fighter at the IAF's frontline base in Adampur in Punjab. The Kargil War had wound down just a week earlier.

I had turned 25 that day.

Over the preceding months, as India successfully evicted Pakistani occupiers from several posts in the heights of North Kashmir, I slogged through the Kargil heights as essentially a cub reporter with NDTV, earning my spurs as a war correspondent – a life goal for a fledgling journalist. I was among a band of young, ridiculously talented reporters who came to define Indian television news: Rajdeep Sardesai, Barkha Dutt, Vikram Chandra, Sreenivasan Jain, Arnab Goswami, Sonia Singh, Suparna Singh, Maya Mirchandani and Sanjay Ahirwal. Ayesha Kagal, an incredible news editor, drove many of my Kargil reports. We were led by Radhika and Prannoy Roy, who let us dream big.

Kargil was India's first televised war. Our phone reports went live on air and our visuals brought Indian viewers together like never before. A dot on the map in North Kashmir became a household name.

Though the war had technically ended by late July, tension remained thick across the region. The IAF stayed on high alert – its pilots, who had clocked close to 1,200 sorties during Operation Safed Sagar, remained ready for action.

The opportunity to fly with the IAF's Mirage pilots was a dream come true. This was unprecedented, a world-exclusive report. No Indian journalist had flown fighter sorties in a war zone before. No one really knew what to expect.

Over the next few days, I flew three sorties on the Mirages. Some of the pilots I flew with would rise to the highest levels of the IAF. Among them was the young Squadron Leader Narmdeshwar Tiwari, who went on to become Vice Chief of the Air Staff, heading the IAF operations during Operation Sindoor.

In the summer of 1999, Mirage 2000s had played a decisive role in winning India the war. Precision laser-guided bomb strikes from the French-built fighters took out Pakistani posts on Tiger Hill – a turning point after which enemy supply routes were targeted at will, severing logistics lines for Pakistani soldiers operating within India's side of the Line of Control (LoC). For Pakistan, this signalled the end of a brief war in which it lost at least 453 soldiers, though some estimates place the actual number closer to 4,000.

What began with a young reporter chasing a dream in 1999 has now returned, full circle, to tell the story of a new generation that has inherited the sky and refuses to yield it.

Those same Mirage 2000s, now significantly upgraded, remain a part of the IAF's sword arm 26 years after Kargil. These same jets struck targets inside Pakistan during Operation Sindoor – the 88-hour mini-war between India and Pakistan that raged from 7 to 10 May 2025.

Adampur, the airbase from where I had flown back in '99, was once again in the thick of action. The S-400 surface-to-air missile system deployed there became the most critical part of the IAF's missile shield during Operation Sindoor, intercepting PAF aircraft while fighting off relentless attacks directed against it.

Little did I know then that those Mirage sorties and my experience in Kargil would lead me into a career as a defence correspondent, covering conflicts around the world – Afghanistan, Iraq, Ukraine, Congo, Siachen, Israel – and reporting on military technology. Aviation, particularly military aviation, has always been an abiding passion.

That flight on the Mirage would be far from my last. I have since flown more than a dozen sorties on fast jets around the world – some of the greatest fighters ever built: the Su-30 MKI, Rafale, Tejas, MiG-29, F-16 Fighting Falcon, F/A-18 Super Hornet, JAS-39 Gripen, MiG-35 and one particularly memorable sortie off the deck of India's aircraft carrier, INS *Viraat*, on a Sea Harrier. These experiences translated into multiple documentaries and news reports.

After three decades of covering the IAF as a journalist and engaging military aviation experts around the world, I felt this was the right time to write this book. When Chiki Sarkar approached me to document Operation Sindoor, I knew exactly what I wanted to focus on – the IAF, its women and men, and the actual conduct of the lethal air battle that broke out between two of the world's premier air forces.

The air war between India and Pakistan was, without question, the most sophisticated air battle fought between near-peer adversaries in decades. Both sides deployed advanced fourth-generation fighter jets, game-changing ultra-long-range air-to-air and surface-to-air missiles and integrated command and control networks that guided the conduct of war on both sides.

I wanted this to be more than a macro-level outline of events – common facts well-established through non-stop media coverage. This needed to be a book on the IAF's war-fighters, bringing out the never-before-told stories of officers who played pivotal roles during Operation Sindoor. What was it like facing a storm of drones overhead? Pressing the launch button of a missile that has never been fired in an Indian war? Mapping a war on the Rectified Air Picture (RAP) screen in real time and making split-second decisions that would impact lives? Because this is the human story of Operation Sindoor.

This project wouldn't have happened without the active assistance of the senior leadership of the IAF, which facilitated interviews with officers, including those honoured with gallantry awards. Those interviews brought unprecedented details – from the moment the order to hit terror camps in Pakistan was issued, to the moment pilots, some already airborne to expand the scope of India's attacks, were ordered to abort their missions and return to base. That happened on 10 May 2025, when Pakistan's Director General of Military Operations came on the hotline at 3.35 p.m. and told his Indian counterpart that Islamabad was interested in a ceasefire, bringing an end to the fighting. Even for someone like me, who had covered every minute of the war, these accounts revealed new layers of the conflict.

First-hand accounts in this book describe pilots mentally preparing for the possibility of being painted (detected) by Pakistani radar when they were seconds away from launching their air-to-surface missiles, the crucial role of S-400 surface-to-air missile units in intercepting high-speed incoming cruise missiles, what top IAF commanders witnessed on screens at their underground IACCS nodes and how IAF base commanders ensured that the mini-townships they led were wholly directed towards the conduct of war when the moment arrived.

India's Operation Sindoor attacks were not a one-way affair. The IAF harbours no illusions about the losses it suffered or what needs to be done in the future to address the threat posed by new-generation weaponry in Pakistan's arsenal and the tactics of an adversary. This book also provides the most in-depth account of why the IAF chose to divulge limited details of the operations during the fighting – which Pakistan referred to as Operation Bunyan-un-Marsoos, its name for the retaliatory counter-offensive against India.

Finally, a significant part of the book focuses on high-resolution satellite imagery that NDTV procured from Maxar (now Vantor). These images showed, in unprecedented detail, the impact of the IAF's strikes on Pakistani bases including Nur Khan, Bholari, Rahim Yar Khan and Murid, among others.

Many of these images, which I first reported on NDTV, have been freshly annotated and reproduced here. The images of the strikes on 10 May provide a vivid picture of how New Delhi was prepared to scale up its military offensive against targets in Pakistan in the face of progressively escalating drone attacks that attempted to saturate IAF defences across a vast arc – from the Siachen Glacier in the north to parts of Gujarat in the south.

There are many lessons to be learnt from Operation Sindoor. I discuss these in the Conclusion, but I wanted to touch upon one here. In spirit, courage, resolve and love for their country, our armed forces are unmatched – from the technician on the ground to the pilot in the sky.

This is their war. Their sky. And through their eyes, I want it to become yours.

Welcome to *The Sky Warriors*.

1

Pahalgam

22 April 2025

It was a bright, glass-clear morning in Pahalgam. The kind of day Kashmir is famous for – sunlight spilling through pine needles, ponies stamping at the trailhead, tourists laughing as they adjusted jackets against the cold wind.

Around 1.30 p.m., the first burst cracked through the air near the wooden fence marking the Baisaran Valley meadow – a concentrated, ripping volley of automatic fire. The sound ricocheted off the limestone cliffs like metallic hail.

The ponies sensed it first. Ears flat, they reared and snapped their tethers, hooves churning the path into mud. Children who had been feeding them apples screamed as the animals bolted towards the treeline.

A mother from Mumbai clutched her six-year-old to her chest and ran, zig-zagging between the white chinar trunks, her dupatta snagging on low branches.

Two to four gunmen – faces partially concealed, olive-green gear over local attire – emerged from the pine cover. They carried M4 carbines and AK-47s. They moved with practised speed.

One attacker raised a hand. The firing paused.

Tourists, perhaps 60 in the open meadow, froze mid-flight. A terrorist ordered people to be separated – on the basis of their religion.

A local pony operator, who attempted to intervene and reason with the militants, was instantly shot.

The segregation took place quickly.

Kashmiri locals and those identified as Muslims were waved away from the main group. The remaining 26 people, Hindus and Sikhs, were forced into a tight semicircle against the split-rail fence that marked the trailhead.

The shooters worked to secure the area. They checked documents to identify the Hindus and Sikhs in the group. One filmed the scene with a body-mounted camera – standard Lashkar-e-Taiba (LeT) protocol. Others used plastic zip-ties to bind the wrists of the victims.

Around 2 p.m., the final volley erupted – a fatal burst. Twenty-six bodies lay in a shallow arc. The attackers escaped immediately, moving quickly towards the dense forest cover.

By 2.45 p.m., the meadow was silent except for ringing phones in the grass.

In the next few hours, the group calling itself the Resistance Front claimed responsibility. Their encrypted statement appeared on the messaging app Telegram, opposing the granting of residency permits to 'outsiders' and threatening that 'violence will be directed towards those attempting to settle illegally.' The same group had claimed responsibility for an attack on a bus carrying Hindu pilgrims, killing at least nine, in Jammu the year before.

The attackers, investigators later discovered, had slipped across the LoC weeks earlier, guided by local handlers who knew every bend of the Lidder River. But these weren't amateurs. They carried sophisticated weapons, night-vision equipment and satellite phones traced back to LeT and Jaish-e-Mohammed (JeM), Pakistan's shadowy proxies.

Among those killed in the attack was IAF Corporal Tage Hailyang, who was on holiday in Pahalgam with his wife. Hailyang reportedly risked his life and guided tourists to safety, helping them escape before he fell to the bullets of the terrorists.

———

At the time, Air Marshal P.K. Vohra was serving as the Senior Air Staff Officer (SASO) of the Western Air Command, one of the IAF's vital operational commands that has an area of responsibility that is strategically significant. It has an awesome responsibility – defending Indian airspace along the International Border (Punjab) and Line of Control (J&K) against Pakistan and the Line of Actual Control to the East, against China, a region contested by three nuclear-armed nations. The Indian Army faces nearly 1.5 million armed troops across these borders. Anything can happen here. At any time. As SASO, Air Marshal Vohra oversaw operations, ensuring readiness through continuous training and exercises for such scenarios.

'The chain of command flows from the Chief of the Air Staff to the AOC-in-C [Air Officer Commanding in Chief] of the operational commands. Each command has Senior Air Staff Officers (SASOs) who exercise their command on individual Air Force stations through Station Commanders. I then ensure stations and units are briefed. I was directly involved in passing orders to the stations, ensuring clarity and execution. It's a structured process, not about speaking directly to squadrons but ensuring the directive reaches the right units,' Air Marshal Vohra says. Every word underlined a system built to function when everything else is collapsing into chaos.

After Pahalgam, Air Marshal Vohra knew that the Western Air Command would be put to the ultimate test. 'Did I think the Indian Air Force was going to be involved in the response? There was no doubt. Absolutely, no doubt.'

This could be war. And it could happen in a matter of days.

2

Preparation

23 April 2025–5 May 2025

When Pahalgam exploded into the headlines, it did more than shock the country – it jolted men out of holiday mode and straight back into uniform. Officers who were on leave did not wait for formal orders from their headquarters. Many packed within hours and came back. Immediately.

'There were guys who called me up who were on leave. They had heard it on the news on the twenty-second. There were guys in Sikkim, there were guys down south. They called me up. They said, "Sir, are you calling us?" I said, "I will call you, don't worry. When the time is right, when it is required." Notwithstanding this, all of them returned within two days. They all came back on their own before we issued the recall. They said, "Sir, we can't sit at home now." So, everybody was eager to have a go, to give a befitting reply. You see, we eat, live, breathe that morning, evening, night. We are like a big family, we always stand together and for us duty and operations trumps everything else, it's our way of life,' said Air Marshal Vohra.

The Air Marshal's alert to units in the Western Air Command came within hours of the Pahalgam attack. 'On 22 April, realising the gruesome nature and scale of the Pahalgam attack, I alerted the Western Air Command units to be ready. When I addressed the Command Headquarters, every station and unit, I told them, keep your gunpowder ready, it is not a question of whether it will happen or not, it is just a question of when. As the Air Force, this is what we practise for, day in and day out. This is no cliché. The only difference is that during training missions, we don't usually load the weapons.' The image of squadrons standing by with loaded ordnance – a stark, menacing readiness – lingered behind the sentence: training made real.

Air Marshal Narmdeshwar Tiwari, the Vice Chief of the Air Staff at the time of Operation Sindoor, was among the first Indian fighter pilots to drop a laser-guided bomb in war. In the visceral months of 1999's Kargil conflict, Air Marshal Tiwari, then a Squadron Leader, flew Mirage 2000s against Pakistani positions on Tiger Hill and Muntho Dhalo, where enemy bunkers crouched above the town of

Dras. The missions he flew then were surgical and decisive: Mirage fighters fitted with Israeli Litening laser-designator pods turned imprecise locations of mountainside bunkers into targetable points on a screen. Those strikes were a pivot – they told the Pakistani Army in no uncertain terms that altitude and isolation were no protection.

Nearly three decades on, Air Marshal Tiwari was plunged into another war with Pakistan. He had only been recently appointed as the Vice Chief of the Air Staff – his first day in his new role was on 1 May, six days before the IAF struck terror targets in Pakistan. Moving from Gandhinagar to New Delhi, he was thrust into top-secret meetings even before he could fully unpack or get his new home ready. There could be war within days, and as the Vice Chief – with a small circle of senior officers – he sat in the hot seat, tasked with carrying out India's mandate to strike terrorist infrastructure across the border.

Meanwhile, the seniormost members of the Army, Navy and Air Force were already bent over maps. Within a day of the attack, Air Marshal A.K. Bharti, Director General of Air Operations, was conferring with Lieutenant General Rajiv Ghai, Director General of Army Operations and Vice Admiral A.N.

Pramod, Director General of Navy Operations. Air Chief Marshal A.P. Singh, along with Air Marshal Tiwari, was present in all meetings when Chief of Army Staff and the Chief of Naval Staff were present. General Anil Chauhan, the Chief of Defence Staff, was often present. By 24 April, they were presenting their plans and a longlist of targets to the Prime Minister. Present at these meetings were Defence Minister Rajnath Singh, the Chief of Defence Staff, the three chiefs of the armed forces and the National Security Advisor Ajit Doval.

In the coming few days, these officers refined their target list, often meeting more than once a day, their deliberations painstakingly moving from strategic intent to the minutest nitty-gritty and every possible scenario of the execution. 'An expected response from Pakistan was calibrated into our plans; it always is. But our thought process was clear – we are not hitting any military targets which lie across the Indo-Pak boundary,' says Air Marshal Bharti. The line was tight: the goal was not escalation for its own sake but a precise, punitive message – to strike terrorist infrastructure without opening a wider front.

From the moment the first strike order went out until Pakistan came to the ceasefire table days later, Air

Marshal Bharti ran the IAF's air battle, monitoring the skies from his command centre where screens pulsed with moving targets. During the Operation Sindoor fighting, he also became the public face of the Air Force, briefing the press and releasing the first videos of Indian hits that the world would see.

India shortlisted nine sites in total to strike. 'It was important that there was a clear message sent,' Air Marshal Vohra noted after the 22 April attack. These locations were key command centres of JeM and LeT, responsible for major attacks like Pulwama (2019) and Mumbai (2008), and now linked to Pahalgam. Four of these targets were located in Pakistan, including Bahawalpur and Muridke, and five were in Pakistan-occupied Kashmir, including Muzaffarabad and Kotli.

The IAF had two primary targets: The first was the Bahawalpur headquarters of JeM led by Masood Azhar. The second was the sprawling 200-acre Markaz-e-Taiba complex in Muridke – the headquarters of Hafiz Saeed's LeT and the public face of its charity wing, Jamaat-ud-Dawa (JuD).

The Muridke and Bahawalpur sites, the IAF knew, 'needed a heavier weight of the attack', according to Air Marshal Bharti – they were strategic hubs, not small outposts located in towns, villages or forests.

Bahawalpur lay approximately 100–150 km west of the India–Pakistan border, near Rajasthan and Punjab, far south of the J&K LoC. Muridke was located 20–30 km from the international border near Lahore. Typically, most Indo-Pak conflicts linked to cross-border terrorism from Pakistan were waged along the LoC.

The Army's seven targets, carefully chosen, were across the LoC and could be destroyed by their weapons. These were:

1. Syedna Bilal Camp, Muzaffarabad – Lashkar-e-Taiba (LeT)
2. Shawai Nallah Camp, Muzaffarabad – Lashkar-e-Taiba (LeT)
3. Kotli Camp – Jaish-e-Mohammed (JeM)
4. Raheel Shahid Camp, Kotli – Hizbul Mujahideen (HM)
5. Ahle Hadith Camp, Bhimber – Lashkar-e-Taiba (LeT)
6. Memoona Joya Camp – Sialkot Hizbul Mujahideen (HM)
7. Sarjal-Tehra Kalan Dett – Gujranwala – Jaish-e-Mohammed (JeM)

The final choices were not the product of a single brain. The targets were picked through what Air

Marshal Bharti describes as a 'collegiate-approach' by key military leaders in the forces. Secrecy was baked into the process: only a handful of senior officers knew the specifics. They were custodians of a plan that, if leaked or misread, could spiral into disaster. As Air Marshal Bharti put it, the plan involved 'preparing for the mission, training hard, maintaining secrecy and sharing information strictly on a need-to-know basis'. When the list of targets landed on his desk, the Director General of Air Operations had just one thought. 'This is our target. It has to be hit. We have to hit it professionally. And that's it.' The language was clinical, almost blunt. The objectives were clear. The execution had to be precise.

As soon as the targets were finalised – the 'when' unknown but inevitable – activity accelerated into a controlled frenzy. Crews rehearsed, weapons were readied, plans were ironed out. The missions were hours, not days away; the choreography had to be perfect.

'We went about contingency planning in terms of what kind of weapons to be used, what are the profiles [of the selected targets] and things like that, and of course, we included a team from Western Air Command as a part of the planning process because the initial strikes, given the pick of the targets, were to largely be done by the Western Air Command. So, we had their core team involved in the planning along with our core teams. So, there were not more than 10 to 15 people in the know of specifics – what are the exact weapons to be used, what are the targets, in the target-sets what are the points to be taken out, which are the squadrons which will be used. Of course, detailed planning had to be done by the people who had to execute the missions. The only thing that we did not tell anyone till a couple of days prior to the strikes was the date and time,' says Air Marshal Tiwari.

Behind every decision, there was a tight lattice of secure communications and guarded movement. There is a particular system that is activated when armed forces go into alert mode – communication protocols are set for everyone. No one is exempted. Aircraft and personnel are moved without as much as a whisper and communication discipline is maintained and ensured at all levels. The Chief, after meetings with political leaders, would come back and brief a small circle; planning continued in scattered venues to minimise risk. Forces were positioned gradually, deliberately; by the morning of 6 May, most people were in place.

Group Captain Sunil Gupta, Commander of an

Akash surface-to-air missile unit, had received orders to deploy forward even earlier. By the time his unit reached their final operational location, they had travelled significant distances from their base through a few state lines, finally to their location – north of Jammu. Moving an Akash battery, with many vehicles and combat units travelling through day and night, was punishing work.

When the order came, 'we just recalled people, whoever was on leave. Everyone joined back,' Gupta said. 'The joining back was also a story – because almost all modes of transport had been stopped [to areas where his missile unit was eventually deployed]. So there were people who shelled out money from their pocket, hitchhiked, climbed atop buses. They have their own stories to tell. This operational location was new to them. But people managed, from all across.'

Like so many military families during the crisis, Group Captain Gupta's wife had no idea where he was or how close to the fighting. 'She had no clue where I was,' he says with a rueful smile.

One of his corporals, in his early twenties, had gotten married at his home in Uttar Pradesh; on the same day, hostilities erupted. Gupta only learnt of the marriage after the ceasefire on 10 May. 'The warrant officers told me that this man . . . got married and reported to duty on the very next day.'

Others pushed through pain. Sergeant Arnav Ahuja*, a specialist driver, saluted Gupta with a visibly swollen finger. Ahuja dismissed it as a sprain. Three days later, it turned out to be a hairline fracture. A fractured finger wouldn't keep Ahuja from his post. Being with the unit when it mattered – that was what counted.

'Mobility itself is fatiguing,' Gupta said. 'You prepare the sites using bulldozers and flatten the ground and you deploy your system. That took a huge toll. Then securing administrative and operational stores, of which you need a regular supply, ensuring movement, communication. That also took a huge amount of energy.'

Like Gupta, Group Captain Manav Bhatia, Commanding Officer of a Sukhoi squadron that would be in the thick of battle, was also on the move early. Within a few days of Pahalgam, the orders came to redeploy his squadron to a forward location. This was one of the many deliberate moves made in the

---

* To protect the privacy and anonymity of the individual involved, name and some identifying details have been changed or omitted.

days between 22 April and 7 May. The ultimate attacks were launched from another base where the squadron shifted to prior to the attack.

The preparations weren't just about logistics. The Chief Operations Officer (COO) of Adampur Airbase in Punjab, which played a massive role during Operation Sindoor, Group Captain A.G. Kumar, knew the PAF was going to come for his base. When Pahalgam happened, like so many officers in the IAF, Kumar felt certain India would respond militarily. And his frontline base in Punjab would be in the thick of it, particularly once Pakistan retaliated. 'My Air Officer Commanding and I told the guys that this time it would be different,' Kumar recalls. 'This was only my personal sense of foreboding. When I told them that Adampur was going to be targeted, it took them a few minutes to believe it.'

The experienced pilot, with 4,200 flight hours under his belt, had a premonition that bordered on certainty. But now his role was larger, more consequential – ensuring that this critical facility, just 100 km from the international border, was prepared for what he believed was inevitable. In the context of Operation Sindoor, he was a backroom man. 'My job was to ensure maintenance, administration and operational support – what we call "raise, train and sustain". But when it comes to actual operations, that's handled by someone who has actual visibility of incoming threats from across the border.'

One of his first jobs after 22 April was to prepare his men psychologically. The IAF's men and women aren't typically deployed right on the border like Army soldiers. 'The Air Force Bases are far from the zone of actual combat, their role and focus in combat is different. It's not the Line of Control, where you hear shots being fired, where artillery exchanges shake the ground around you. At IAF bases, you may be 80, 100 km away from the border, unlike the Army that is positioned right on the border to take on immediate threats such as infiltration attempts or responding to cross-border shelling. The IAF is exposed to a different aspect of warfare. The main goal is to prepare equipment for battle, ensure finer details are sorted while at the same time being prepared for sudden strikes by the enemy with barely any warning. It's a different readiness mindset.' But if his base was hit with missiles or bombs, the impact would be just as devastating as any engagement along the Indo-Pak boundary. The air warriors under his command needed to understand this. They needed to be ready.

'Listen, we need to get ready for whatever we have practised for. There are high chances that we are going to get hit. We told them that bombs could fall on them. They could see people dying. Maybe somebody would not come back from a mission. Others might get an arm or a leg blown off. But they had to be resilient and continue … It takes time to get people into the correct frame of mind.' The mental preparation would come in handy during 8 and 9 May when Adampur became the focus for the PAF.

The date and time were finally confirmed between 4 May and 5 May – 13 days after Pahalgam. Air Chief Marshal A.P. Singh had been running a continual round of briefings in New Delhi with Defence Minister Rajnath Singh, the National Security Advisor Ajit Doval, and sometimes Prime Minister Narendra Modi and Home Minister Amit Shah. The Air Force had latitude in how to conduct strikes once targets were set. But the timing 'was the decision of the Government. The target sets were known to us about a week before. But the exact date and time [for the strikes to go in] was decided at the national leadership level,' says Air Marshal Tiwari.

Air Chief Marshal A.P. Singh called in his Vice Chief and a handful of others for an urgent briefing.

Air Marshal Tiwari says he 'had a sense of what was coming'. The Chief had been in long high-level meetings during the day, and then he met us. 'It was held at one of the places where few of us met for discussions, the Chief sat down and told us specifically that the date and time has been fixed. It was not dramatic – just in a calm, matter of fact way.'

When the order finally arrived – the locked set of targets, the precise day and time – the Air Force moved from preparing to doing. Air Marshal Tiwari described the transition without melodrama but with the intensity of someone who has done it before: 'I think since there had been so much anticipation, we were practically ready to go in on any day.' The announcement brought a strange finality: 'a sense of finiteness – that yes, now it's going to happen'.

From then on there was no room for doubt – only the mechanics of execution: weapons checks, briefings, navigation, mission planning. As Air Marshal Tiwari, the Vice Chief, put it plainly, training, discipline and adherence to procedures carried them through. 'When you go into operations, you don't treat it as something entirely new, if you do, one will get overwhelmed by the occasion. That should not happen. The only thing different here is you are actually going with a live weapon.'

The task of planning the 7 May strikes did not come as a bolt out of the blue to the forces, but rather as the culmination of years of surveillance and training. It is for such contingencies that the IAF prepares for as a professional organisation, this is what every IAF personnel is trained and groomed for, from the day he or she joins service. 'We have been watching these targets for years. And we were ready with the weapons, with the targets, with the aircraft, with trained pilots,' says Air Marshal Vohra.

When final mission orders came, with him as a part of the strike package, Group Captain Manav Bhatia, who commanded a Sukhoi squadron, knew that this was the moment. 'My first thought was, okay, it's time. I am ex-NDA [National Defence Academy]. I joined the forces in June 1999. [I did] three years at the NDA, one year at the Air Force Academy and 20 years of service. [Through that time] you are getting airborne [virtually] every day. You are training to press that trigger on the day that it matters. You are training so hard because on that day, you cannot fail.'

Air Marshal Bhatia's and Air Marshal Vohra's words were echoed by Air Marshal Bharti and every member of the IAF interviewed for this book. 'We knew the targets [which were ultimately assigned] well – Bahawalpur and Muridke – having monitored them for years via ISR [intelligence, surveillance, reconnaissance] and satellite imagery. We were ready with aircraft, pilots and weapons. When the orders came, it was a matter of execution, not anxiety. We knew the implications of hitting these high-value targets and were prepared for escalation.'

What began akin to a routine night training sortie ultimately ended up becoming small, exact legends in service histories: planes slicing into hostile airspace, ordnance finding its marks, the quiet arithmetic of damage assessments, and – on the other side – a political leadership that had chosen a measured but unmistakable reply. The narrative of Pahalgam did not end with grief; it resulted in a nation's military machine converting grief into action, and for a small number of men and women, to measure, precisely and professionally, the cost of sending a clear message that could be heard far and wide – India will respond to terror strikes on its soil.

3

The Wait

6 May 2025

On 6 May, less than five hours before the IAF and Indian Army launched their strikes on the Pakistani terror targets, the Commander of an Integrated Air Command and Control System was at a birthday party. The Node Commander was an experienced combat specialist who had commanded a fighter squadron among other things. A young flying officer under his command had just turned 23, and the room felt like any other off-duty evening: cake, jokes, the sense of a normal day clocking out. Little did the men and women at this party know that the IAF was about to go to war. And that their unit would be in the thick of action.

The Node Commander was the man who stood between a glowing screen and the weapons that could reach across hundreds of kilometres. He commanded one of the IAF's Integrated Air Command and Control System (IACCS) nodes – a state-of-the-art, highly automated brain hidden in an underground facility. One of the many in service, this node was part of a national grid watching every inch of the air picture – military and civilian – and sweeping far beyond India's borders when required. It ensured seamless sharing of information, not only to IAF operations centres, but if required, also to Navy and Army units.

An IACCS node is much more than a simple radar-monitoring outpost. It is a digitally networked command nerve centre where radar echoes, satellite data and airborne feeds are stripped of noise, fused and projected as a single living image: the Rectified Air Picture (RAP). The IACCS is the cornerstone of the IAF's networked air defence strategy. Each node commander of the IAF, a senior officer, has the authority to direct the launch of weapons that may be physically located hundreds of kilometres away. The Node Commander was the senior officer at a crucial node that looked after the defence of a large part of North India along with support from additional IAF nodes further south.

Officers won't disclose the precise location, but they will describe the room. 'Have you seen the movie *Apollo 13*? The operations room seems to be a replica of Mission Control in *Apollo 13*. We used to keep joking that we are the Houston of the Indian Air Force. It's a fairly big room and we have a data wall – a big screen in front. The Air Battle Manager (ABM) and the Sector Director sit at a vantage point along with another key officer so that they get better visibility of the screen as well as what is happening below where several controllers worked on individual consoles. In the Node Commander's Ops Room, the IACCS node, the RAP glowed on the huge data wall; officers watched it like lifeguards watching a crowded sea. The node received continuous inputs from multiple radars, civil aviation sensors, observation posts and, when airborne, airborne early warning and control (AEW&C) system planes. Algorithms reconciled conflicting tracks, tagged every blip with identity and intent and handed a common picture to fighters, surface-to-air missile units and counter-drone systems.

From the Node Commander's chair, that picture was not just information, it was also communication. The node 'facilitates secure, real-time exchange of voice, data and imagery, ensuring near-instant coordination between aircraft, missile batteries and ground stations,' he explained. When a track turned hostile, the node could trigger a layered engagement: long-range interceptors, medium-range missiles and close-in point defence. Described by Air Marshal Bharti as the 'unsung heroes' of Operation Sindoor, the IACCS also tracked and neutralised Pakistani drones. The Army's Akshateer network served as a capable sensor for seamless 'sensor to shooter' response within the overall system.

The officer in command of the node had the full picture. Redundancy is built into the architecture. If a node were knocked out or went offline, its entire suite of functions – the weapons control, the fighter coordination, the threat picture – would instantly transfer to another node.' The system could not be decapitated.

The nodes were not operating alone. Above ground, at one of the Western Air Command's many Ops rooms, Air Marshal Tiwari watched the broader chessboard, maintaining command over operations. The Node Commander handled immediacy – the hands on the controls in his IACCS node – Air Marshal Tiwari was one of the minds that had stitched the information given by the nodes into a campaign. He and other senior commanders had shortlisted targets, weighed escalation and calibrated the political and military decision to strike. From his vantage, the RAP continued to feed data for the conduct of bigger meetings with the national leadership, influencing the timing that would turn planning into action.

After Pahalgam, the Node Commander had expected a limited response. 'I thought that the action would be limited. That was inherent in my mind; that is how the response to terrorism had been earlier. I felt that we were talking of only the LoC region. So when I came to know that one of the targets in my area of responsibility had been picked, which I had not anticipated, it surprised me. And we were going to be in the thick of it. I called my number two and also my COO. We discussed what would happen, what we needed to do and how to go about it. And for a week after that, we carried on as normal.'

On the day of the attack, the Node Commander remained calm. 'We didn't want anybody else to know that "the day [for the attack] is today". So, the rest of the activities happened as routine. Nobody other than the three of us knew and we made our checklists [for impending military action] without letting anybody know. In fact, one of the youngsters [in the unit] made a comment [at the party] that the Commanding Officer [serving under the Node Commander] was late coming for the cake-cutting, which generally doesn't happen. So they started saying, "Something is going to happen."'

The Node Commander's unit was operational 24 hours a day, 365 days a year. Accordingly, the officers scheduled for the next shift had about an hour after the cake-cutting ceremony, which was scheduled for 7.00 p.m., to return to their posts to prepare for what they were told were pre-planned night-flying operations from one of the forward airbases in the West.

The Node Commander's planned deception – to pretend everything was normal – continued till late in the evening. Under normal circumstances, the node operates on shifts, one of which ends late in the evening. An hour later, once he was sure that the shift changeover had happened, the Node Commander shut the doors of the Ops Room, not wanting any more movement of people coming in and going out. 'That started giving an inkling to people that something was going to happen tonight.' Officers on a previous shift who had not left till then were getting ready to leave for the day. But by then, all movement had been frozen. The doors were shut. You had to remain at your positions.

At 11.00 p.m., as the clock ticked away towards the launch of the strikes, one of the men who was not feeling well wanted to report sick at the medical facility at the base. 'You're not going,' said the Node

Commander. The man ended up remaining in the Ops Room till 2.30 a.m. before he was allowed to leave. By this time, the operation had begun and the necessary element of secrecy was over.

Inside the underground IACCS node, the hours afterwards blurred into a state of submarine-like endurance. By the time Pakistan came to the ceasefire table on 10 May, the Node Commander had been in the Ops Room for 64 hours straight – 'fuelled by caffeine pills, snatching only slivers of sleep. I slept for the first time on 10 May. I took naps for two–three hours before that.' Cut off from news and daylight, his team lost track of time. 'It was like being in a submarine. The same level of light [at the node] through the day, the same level of darkness throughout the day. The same air that you are breathing. My COO and I reached the stage when we had to look at a computer screen to figure out what date and time it was and whether it was time for lunch or for dinner.'

Above ground, the IAF's physical instruments – fighters, sensors and missiles – were the tools that the node and command used to convert intent into effect. Key officers trooped into the Western Air Command's Ops Room, expecting another drill, another rehearsal. It was not.

'At a certain time on 6 May, I called in the key people into the Ops Room,' says Air Marshal Vohra. 'We were doing it every day. We used to call people and continuously keep going over our drills and training. So, on that day also, I [had] called in key officers. Nobody knew that "we were going today". I had issued the orders to the stations and to the squadrons a few hours before. [It was now that] I told everyone in the Ops Room. There was a buzz of excitement all across. Our air defence units were set up, our strikes were set up.'

What followed was the choreography of machines and men. Fighters were readied, air-to-air missiles and air-to-surface munitions loaded, flight plans sealed.

Like the Node Commander, Air Marshal Vohra also strove for business-as-usual on 6 May, acting as if it were any other day. Even hours before launch, the façade of calm held. 'When it happened, I must tell you that we made a lot of effort to normalise things. We had decided that we would not extend working hours at the headquarters. This is because if a large number of people are staying at headquarters one night, then people expect something to happen. So we went about our tasks in a normal way, as we had been doing the previous days. I had just moved into

Delhi, and since I was staying some distance away, I had already told my [vehicle] to come and pick me up at a designated time. I didn't want to arrive at headquarters before time because that would again raise [eyebrows].' It was just business as usual.

When the orders to strike Pakistan came in a day before the actual attack, Group Captain Bhatia assembled his pilots in the squadron crew-room. There was no podium from which he addressed them. Instead, the men huddled together – in a spirit of camaraderie. Each pilot sensed that something big was going to be announced. When Bhatia broke the news, there was no formality – just simple orders passed on to pilots who would back each other – to death if needed.

'The scene of the crew-room was very informal. We were just standing next to each other. The hierarchy that exists during office hours went. Now, the guy standing next to you will be the guy who will be your wing man. And he will make sure you are safe before he turns back [from a mission]. I was aware of my [attack] mission – I briefed them on the formation: "Okay guys, this is the first formation. So you and you, you and you [will go]." And then the other guys ask, "Sir, why not me?" So I say, "Don't worry. *Aur mauke aa rahe hain* [More opportunities are coming]."'

Down in his IACCS node several hundred kilometres away, the Node Commander waited, watching the RAP like a man watching a tideline – not yet sure when the wave would break, but certain that it would. Consoles glowed in various colours, each colour representing specifics; voices chirped in clipped, rehearsed cadences; data links ferried in critical information about the mission. Outside, the city breathed the shallow, ordinary breath of night.

He felt the familiar, old chord of readiness – the same that twangs, resonant, before any launch: nervy, disciplined, strangely intimate. A clock on the shelf ticked towards an hour that had been chosen elsewhere, in rooms of higher counsel. In those last minutes there was no bravado, no swagger – only waiting and the small ceremonies of preparation.

The line between plan and action trembled and held. They were ready. They had done what they could. Now they waited for the hour to fall.

4

The Battle Begins

7 May 2025, 1.05 a.m.

Group Captain Kunal Kalra, a Sukhoi-30 MKI pilot and the Flight Commander of his squadron, was in the air, on an attack mission.

It was shortly after 12 a.m. on 7 May 2025 and he was flying in the front seat of the Russian-designed fighter. The pilot in the rear cockpit was his Weapons Systems Operator on this mission.

He had orders to attack a high-value terror target in Pakistan, among the first targets to be struck in the early hours of 7 May. His jet was one among a host of IAF fighters in the air and manoeuvring to get into position to launch what would be the deepest strikes on Pakistani soil since the 1971 war.

It was not all smooth sailing. There were challenges that had to be overcome.

His attack mission – right till the point when he fired his air-to-surface missile – had to be flown in a very specific manner to be successful. While flying, he had to penetrate a wall of dense, heavy cumulonimbus clouds. These are often described as tall mountain-like clouds which can produce severe weather conditions – thunderstorms, lightning, thunder and heavy rain. This was the last thing Kalra needed as he sped towards his missile launch window. 'There was a lot of clouding and we didn't have a chance to deviate because that would have given our flight path details to the adversary. So we continued with what we had and penetrated some amount of weather,' he says, his terse words belying the challenges he faced.

Other fighters in his squadron were close by – but there was zero communication within the formation. Total radio silence. Each and every pilot knew what they were up against. If it wasn't the weather, it could soon be missiles fired from Pakistani fighters or surface-to-air missile units.

Kalra and the pilots around him pressed on when, suddenly, a red master caution light, lit up in his cockpit display. An aural alert – a woman's voice steady and mechanical – sounded simultaneously, telling him that his Su-30 had an electrical system error. In a situation like this, Kalra's peacetime orders were clear – return to the base. Let technicians address the problem. But today was not an ordinary day.

'Knowing that the aircraft is capable of launching the weapon, I took a decision to launch despite the challenges I faced.'

As he flew to his designated launching point, Kalra could see dots in the sky. Other fighters in his formation had started launching their missiles targeting the heart of Pakistan's terror network.

With missiles flying all around him, it would have been a huge challenge for Kalra to visually pick up any missile which may have been headed his way.

'If a missile is fired in your direction, all you can see are the dots which glow in the night and rapidly grow very fast in size [if they approach you]. They come right at you before you can even think of reacting. So you have to [be alert].' All this happens in a just a few seconds.

The stakes couldn't have been higher. The pilot was working in pitch darkness, in poor weather conditions with no real visual reference. And all this with a serious electrical fault. Later he would learn that he and his formation had, in fact, been fired on by the PAF.

Kalra reached his optimum launch position. An aural warning sounded and a single word appeared on the Head-Up Display on the transparent screen of his cockpit – *launch*. He pressed the trigger on his control stick. There was a slight judder as the missile left the pylon of the wing. The missile's rocket motor ignited in moments. And the sky lit up. It was 1.05 a.m.

'When the missile goes, it is orangish. The sky is lit up. It was a dark night and it was not dark anymore. And you know that this missile is going to do some damage and the nation's hope is being carried on it.'

The missile launched by Kalra was 'fire and forget'. Once launched, the missile knew where to fly – its microprocessors calculating its time to impact, plotting its course, tracking its trajectory as it soared through the sky into Pakistani airspace.

But Kalra's job was not over.

He had another missile for a second target. Which is when he encountered another technical issue unconnected to the electrical glitch he was experiencing. This time, it was a problem with his weapons system. His air-to-surface missile would not launch until this was resolved. Time was running out. He needed to be in position to launch – normally just two to three minutes of flying time away.

'Launch of the second weapon was a priority while following all safety norms. I knew that this was not that urgent that I could not hold for another five minutes. I took a calculated call at that time to reset my weapon system. If I was able to launch in five minutes, I would launch. If this cutoff was not met, then of course I would have to return to fly another day.'

He took the decision to continue with his mission despite clear danger all around him. The Sukhoi is among the largest fighter jets in the world – relatively easy to pick up on enemy radar. The longer he lingered, the more likely was the prospect of being shot down. You are under greater threat after the first weapon has been fired,' says Kalra. Pakistani radars could have been alerted by the launch of his first missile and efforts to target his aircraft would have been persistent.

'My entire formation had fired and I was left, since I had been dealing with some issues. If the enemy were to obtain a lock-on to my aircraft, a missile would definitely be launched, which is why the window of opportunity [to fire the second missile] was very limited.'

By this time there could have been other problems, potentially life-threatening ones which could emerge. His Sukhoi being painted by enemy radar was a possibility. If this happened, the enemy would know where he was and they could have attempted to lock on to his jet, before attempting a missile launch at Kalra. There could, in fact, be a hostile missile launch targeting him at any moment.

In such a situation, Kalra's radar warning receiver – his key sensor that is meant to warn him about enemy radar activity directed at his fighter would light up.

He would have to throw his jet into a desperate evasive manoeuvre to evade the missiles targeting him. Evasive manoeuvres are last-ditch, high-G actions a fighter pilot executes when radar warning receivers scream 'lock' and 'missile launch'.

The pilot instantly rolls his jet and pulls into a maximum-rate break turn (7 to 9-plus Gs), perpendicular to the incoming missile in order to minimise radar return and break the missile's tracking. Simultaneously, the pilot jinks violently up and down, if necessary dumping dense chaff clouds and flares while cranking hard to try and force the missile to overshoot. In darkness or when flying in clouds or bad weather, flying is purely done on instruments; the horizon disappears, the G-suit inflates painfully and the airframe groans, strained to its limits. The goal: bleed the missile's energy, deny its seeker a clean solution, and survive the next 20–40 seconds until the rocket motor burns out. Split-second timing, raw physical endurance and pure instinct decide life or death, staying or ejecting if your fighter is hit. 'You have to take evasive action irrespective, because you have seen it and it could come and hit you. In modern air warfare, the missile of choice in targeting an enemy fighter is highly sophisticated. These are beyond-visual range air-to-air missiles, fast and extremely accurate. 'They climb higher and then they come down, so you have to take action so that these dots [that you may see] are not on you,' Kalra says calmly, remembering only the focused calculations he made, while sifting away the tension and threat.

Given the technical issues that Kalra had been encountering on his aircraft, a scenario where he could be engaged by enemy missiles was a worst-case scenario. In the fast and extremely complex scenario that he found himself in, Kalra would have some tough choices to make. He would have seconds to make them.

However, persistence paid off for Kalra and his Weapons Systems Operator, they were able to launch, and immediately streak away beyond the firing range of the Pakistani aircraft.

It had been a close call.

The operation that Kalra was a key part of was a success. In the 7 May strikes in the early morning, the Indian Army and the IAF achieved their goal – targeting LeT, JeM and HM facilities and eliminating nine major terror launchpads. In a detailed statement on 14 May, after the fighting ended, the government stated that 'over 100 terrorists were killed as a result of the strikes' on that day. A number of high-profile terrorists on India's most-wanted list were also killed in a single night, crippling key modules. They included Yusuf Azhar, Abdul Malik Rauf and Mudassir Ahmad, all of whom were linked to the IC-814 hijack of 1999 and the 2019 Pulwama blast.

The government's Press Information Bureau press release of 14 May summed up the radical nature of the strike. 'India redefined the rules of engagement, striking deep into Pakistan's heartland, including its Punjab province and Bahawalpur, once considered out of bounds even for US drones. India made it clear: neither the LoC nor Pakistani territory will remain untouched if terror originates from there . . . Operation Sindoor drew a new red line – if terror is state policy, it will be met with a visible and forceful response. This marked a shift from deterrence to direct action.'[10]

'This was an absolutely flawlessly executed strike,' said Air Marshal Bharti of the IAF operation. Seated in the IAF Command and Control Centre in New Delhi, he was seeing a real-time feed of the air battle as it commenced.

'We watched the targets being hit in real time,' he recalls. 'It was a major moment of success, confirming we'd struck Bahawalpur and Muridke precisely.'

Bomb damage assessment (BDA) is the military's way of looking back in time moments after a missile strikes. Satellite imagery, drones, reconnaissance aircraft and ground reports feed into its algorithms to estimate what exactly has been destroyed – buildings, convoys or people. That night, the assessments left little doubt: both sites were hit more than once, the damage severe.

Soon after the strikes, shortly after 1 a.m., Lieutenant General Rajiv Ghai, India's Director General of Military Operations (DGMO) reached for the hotline he used to call the Pakistani DGMO every Tuesday. Established after the 1971 war and formalised in the 1990s, the hotline was used by the two DGMOs to prevent escalation along the LoC. Tonight, the conversation was different. Ghai's message to his Pakistani counterpart, Major General

Kashif Abdullah, was clinical – New Delhi had struck only terror bases, not civilians, not the Pakistani military. There would be no escalation. India's carefully worded press release, released at 1.44 a.m., echoed his words. 'Our actions have been focused, measured and non-escalatory in nature. No Pakistani military facilities have been targeted. India has demonstrated considerable restraint in selection of targets and method of execution.'

The impact on the ground, however, was clear.

India's precision strikes on terrorist camps in Pakistan, including key sites in Muridke (Lashkar-e-Taiba's Markaz Taiba) and Bahawalpur (Jaish-e-Mohammed's Jamia Masjid Subhan Allah) inflicted significant physical damage to infrastructure associated with militant training and operations, as confirmed by satellite imagery and ground reports.

In Muridke, the sprawling Markaz Taiba complex – spanning multiple buildings for arms training, physical conditioning, and radicalisation – suffered extensive structural devastation. Four buildings, including the administration block, were demolished: roofs sagged dangerously with large holes allowing sunlight through, doors were blown inward by blasts, and the ground was littered with debris.

The adjacent Jamia Ummul Qurah mosque sustained partial roof collapse and large gaping missile-induced holes in the ceiling. Missile fragments, reportedly still hot and emitting explosive odours, were recovered on-site.

Two large nearby buildings, a part of the complex, were obliterated, scattering solar panels and broken bricks.

In Bahawalpur, 100 km inside Pakistan, the Jamia Masjid Subhan Allah – serving as JeM's headquarters for training, indoctrination, and leadership residences – was reduced to rubble.

Post-strike satellite images showed gaping holes in the mosque's dome, collapsed surrounding structures, and widespread debris across the site.

Video footage captured bright flashes during the strikes, confirming direct hits on buildings used for arms and religious training.

India's strikes on Pakistani terror infrastructure were heavy and precise. Collateral damage was not visible in satellite imagery or in extensive video of the targets which were struck. This had been the stated goal in Operation Sindoor – to strike Pakistani terror hubs, without targeting their military or causing civilian casualties.

The response on the other side was anything but resistant.

Islamabad, it seemed, had already made its choice. The calculus had shifted. What India intended as a statement of surgical intent would be portrayed by Pakistan as an act of war. The restraint Delhi promised would not be reciprocated. The skies over the subcontinent, quiet now in the predawn darkness, would not remain so for long.

5

Pakistan Attacks

7 May 2025, 1.05–2.00 a.m.

Pakistan's response was quick, the PAF fighters got airborne soon after the IAF and Indian Army were hitting the terror targets. The IAF had been watching them closely. 'Pakistani air activity and ground activity were under constant surveillance,' says Air Marshal Bharti. After the Pahalgam attack of 22 April, Pakistani squadrons had been flying with unusual frequency. Yet, even with that heightened alert, the immediacy of their reaction did not appear normal to Indian planners.

As he stood before a wall of screens, a dangerous picture presented itself to Air Marshal Bharti. Symbols representing airborne fighter aircraft danced across a digital map of the subcontinent. A larger number of PAF fighter aircraft had begun to appear in the sky. In the underground node, the Node Commander watched dozens of enemy aircraft light up the screens across the border. Indian fighters, already airborne on combat air patrol, mirrored the pattern – each symbol on the radar a possible duel waiting to happen. At least 50 Pakistani fighters faced off with India's patrols.

The airspace above Punjab and Jammu was alive with the roar of engines and the red and orange glow of afterburners, with the two air forces staring each other down in darkness. By 1.25 a.m., the first Pakistani missiles – air-to-air and possibly surface-to-air – were fired.

The Indian jets had held their line inside national airspace; none crossed the LoC or international border. But they were within the range of Pakistan's missiles. There were instances of transmission losses and silence adding to concerns.

However, clarity emerged on the evolving air picture. Pakistani missiles were detected in the air and more were being launched. The IAF's command network flipped into combat mode. Rules of engagement shifted to 'weapons free' (shoot at will).

'The moment it was clear that he was firing at us, the rules of engagement were permissive to start firing at him,' says the Node Commander. Air Marshal Tiwari entered the IAF ops centre, as the air battle commenced. 'It was pretty intense,' he says in his usual understated style, giving a sense of the atmosphere in the command centre.

In an instant, the night sky over the subcontinent turned into a theatre of war. In IACCS node and in other operations centres that mirrored the image the Node Commander was seeing, the screens glowed with missile tracks; every officer watching knew what it meant. Despite efforts made by India's Director General of Military Operations to reach out to his Pakistani counterpart, Islamabad had dragged India into a full-fledged conflict. The escalation in fighting that happened over the next couple of days was perhaps inevitable.

As the action unfolded, Air Marshal Tiwari could see the IAF was responding as per the plan. 'I was monitoring on the screen. It is very difficult to sit there and start getting involved in the tactical battle. Things were already happening. The commands [Western and South-Western Air Commands] had already made a plan. And they were going as per the plan. Of course, the main execution was being coordinated by the nodes.'

'What I recall was that there was a big group [of Pakistani aircraft] in the north opposite Jammu and Kashmir, there was one in the centre [Adampur and Pathankot] and one further south towards Bhatinda, Suratgarh and Nal. These were the three major pockets that I recall on the screen. They were not very active towards the south in the direction of Karachi. There are many occasions when you see a number of aircraft, so at any given point of time, there were about 50 aircraft across [the international border and Line of Control] and a similar number on our side.'

The PAF fielded its mix of Chinese-built J-10CE and JF-17 fighters, backed by US F-16s – the backbone of its fleet for decades. The PAF is believed to have launched multiple rounds of PL-15 air-to-air missiles – among the most advanced in China's arsenal.

Inducted into service just three years before, the J-10CE was an export derivative of the J-10C, and strategically positioned as Pakistan's counter to India's formidable Rafale fleet. As Pakistan's premier fighter aircraft, it integrated speed, manoeuvrability and formidable avionics.[11]

The threat, however, came from its advanced active electronically scanned array (AESA) radar, capable of detecting Indian aircraft at extended ranges while simultaneously tracking numerous targets with precision. When coupled with the long-range PL-15 beyond-visual-range (BVR) air-to-air missile, the J-10CE emerged as a formidable and adaptable asset, equally proficient in air combat and precision ground-attack missions.

The PL-15, one among a new generation of Chinese BVR air-to-air missiles, can strike targets at extreme ranges, thereby changing the nature of air warfare over the subcontinent. Propelled to velocities exceeding Mach 5 – five times the speed of sound – the PL-15 is believed to be capable of striking adversary aircraft at distances surpassing 200 km, equivalent to striking a target in Delhi from Agra.[12]

The PL-15 has a dual-pulse engine that fires twice during flight – once at launch and again midway - keeping it fast and making it almost impossible for enemy pilots to escape. It can also receive updated targeting information from other sources (like ground radars), allowing it to chase targets even before its own radar can see them.

Later in the war, India's Armed Forces were also able to locate unexploded Chinese PL-15s in fields in Punjab – an intelligence coup which will now enable the IAF to plan operations against perhaps the most advanced air-to-air missile in Pakistan's arsenal.

During the four days of the operation, both sides took hits. Each claimed victories, each denied losses. On social media, self-styled analysts would begin counting kills like cricket scores. Anonymous posts, doctored images, grainy videos – the online battle for national pride began before the real one had even ended.

'All I can say is that we have achieved the objectives we selected, and all our pilots are back home,' Air Marshal Bharti told reporters – his phrasing deliberate, offering reassurance but not elaborating further.

Independent satellite imagery, ground reports from Pakistan and official Indian claims – backed by publicly released videos of IAF and Indian Army strikes going through made it evident that the attacks on terror-training camps in Pakistan were entirely successful.

India targeted infrastructure of groups like Lashkar-e-Taiba (LeT) and Jaish-e-Mohammed (JeM), with standout impacts at LeT's Markaz Taiba in Muridke and JeM's Markaz Subhan Allah in Bahawalpur.

In Muridke, in the Punjab province, about 30 km north of Lahore and 18–25 km inside Pakistani territory – the sprawling Markaz Taiba complex had served as the LeT's primary headquarters. Established in 2000 and spanning over 200 acres, it included training facilities for arms handling, physical conditioning, intelligence operations, and ideological indoctrination.

Perpetrators of the 2008 Mumbai attacks, including Ajmal Kasab, received training here. Osama bin Laden reportedly funded parts of the complex, including a mosque and guesthouse.

The strikes hit with clinical accuracy: multiple missiles appear to have impacted over several minutes, demolishing key structures. Post-strike satellite imagery from Maxar Technologies revealed extensive devastation – roofs collapsed with large penetration holes, administration blocks reduced to debris-strewn ruins, and adjacent buildings like the Jamia Ummul Qura mosque showing partial dome collapse and blast-induced craters.

Ground reports described scattered shrapnel, blown-in doors, and obliterated residential sections, with solar panels and bricks littering the site. Four primary impact points targeted operational hubs, leaving surrounding areas largely intact to minimise collateral effects.

This destruction disrupted the LeT's core training and radicalisation capabilities, long a 'terror nursery' despite international sanctions.

Further south in Bahawalpur – approximately 100

km inside Pakistan and the deepest penetration of the operation – the Markaz Subhan Allah complex functioned as JeM's operational headquarters.

Spread across 15–18 acres along the Karachi-Torkham Highway, it housed a mega-mosque (Jamia Masjid Subhan Allah), leadership residences, and facilities for youth recruitment, fundraising, arms training and religious indoctrination.

Founded by Masood Azhar, a Bahawalpur native, the site remained active despite UN designations, hosting anti-India rhetoric and planning.

Indian forces employed advanced munitions for direct hits. Satellite before-and-after comparisons showed dramatic transformation: three of the mosque's domes pierced or collapsed, creating gaping holes while two remained untouched, demonstrating precision.

Surrounding structures spanning over 2,100 square metres lay in rubble, with bright flashes captured on video confirming multiple explosions. Debris fields expanded across the compound, reducing key indoctrination and command buildings to heaps.

Reports indicated heavy damage to residences linked to JeM leadership, disrupting fundraising and cadre mobilisation.

The operation, completed in about 25 minutes using air- and ground-launched assets from Indian soil, avoided military installations.

It neutralised significant terrorist infrastructure, reportedly eliminating over 100 militants across sites. Physical evidence – craters, structural collapses, and debris – underscored the strikes' effectiveness in degrading long-standing terror hubs deep in Pakistani Punjab, a rare escalation since 1971.

While rebuilding efforts emerged later under various pretexts, the immediate devastation markedly impaired operational capacities of LeT and JeM.

Asked why the IAF would not confirm figures, Air Marshal Tiwari was crystal clear and blunt.

'No country in the world gives you an official confirmation of losses – you give me one example,' he said. 'Anything we say either confirms or denies the claims the adversary has been talking of, and we don't want to do either. In long-range engagements there is always that element of doubt – have you hit or not hit? Confirming either way would be an advantage to your adversary. The same thing is true of them – they've not confirmed any of their losses. Nobody seems to be asking them. Pakistan is building a narrative which they are comfortable with and our people tend to fall into that trap 'If you just go back in history – in World War II, between the US and UK they lost more than twice the number of aircraft as the Luftwaffe, yet they came out victorious. They lost almost 150,000-plus aircraft. The aggressor always has losses because he goes in harm's way. The PAF has always had a defensive mindset. For us, the primacy of the Air Force is the strike force. Therefore, when you go in harm's way, there will be damages and losses. The numbers are definitely much lower than what Pakistan has claimed, but we don't want to give official confirmations. That's our stand – and it remains consistent. Pakistan has suffered heavy losses on the ground, which it won't talk about.'

As soon as they detected Pakistani air-to-air missiles flying towards them and were ordered by ground controllers guiding the air battle, IAF jets moved away from the kill-zone of Pakistani missiles. For now, the IAF would rely on its missile shield – helmed by the Russian-built S-400, a long-range surface-to-air missile system, which had already started locking onto and engaging Pakistani jets in the sky. If the S-400 failed, there were other state-of-the-art surface-to-air missile systems deployed in a staggered manner – including the Israeli-designed medium-range surface-to-air missile (MR-SAM), also known as the Barak 8, the made-in-India Akash, and the Israeli SpyDer and Russian Pechora for more close-in engagements.

'Our first reaction was to keep ourselves safe and so we pulled our guys a little bit back. But we gave freedom to our surface-to-air missile guys.'

'This was the optimal scenario,' says Air Marshal Tiwari. 'Our S-400, Akash and MR-SAM systems engaged effectively.'

In Adampur Airbase, Group Captain Animesh Patni was in the hot seat in the early hours of 7 May, helming firing units of one of the IAF's most prized possessions – the Russian-built S-400 'Triumf' surface-to-air missile system designed to intercept even ballistic missiles.

This Russian-made surface-to-air missile system, known as 'S-400', became one of the heroes of Operation Sindoor. Approved for acquisition in 2015, the IAF placed an order worth ₹40,000 crore – $5.43 billion – for five S-400 regiments (sets of radar systems, multiple batteries, launchers and a command and control centre). India did this knowing fully well it risked sanctions from the United States under the Countering America's Adversaries Through Sanctions Act (CAATSA).[13]

Washington threatened consequences for countries engaging in significant transactions with Russian defence firms. New Delhi, which considers strategic autonomy the cornerstone of its foreign policy, chose military capability over diplomatic fallout. The order went through.

The S-400 is a highly mobile, long-range surface-to-air missile system capable of intercepting stealth aircraft, cruise missiles, ballistic missiles and drones. In use with Russia since 2007, it is widely recognised as superior to comparable systems like the US Patriot in terms of versatility and target-engagement capacity. The integrated system can track 300 targets at a time and launch missiles against 36 at a time. It does so at speeds up to Mach 14 (17,000 km/hour), with an advertised response time of under 10 seconds.[14]

With missiles flying across the international border, Patni knew he could be called into action in minutes.

He was. Patni was ordered to fire. Weapons free, engage targets. It was a scenario that he had trained for time and time again, but always with his formidable weapons system in safe mode – the missiles would not leave their launchers. The radars and systems would simulate incoming threats. And kills would not be real.

But this was the real deal.

Actively monitoring the air-picture around him through the data-linked IACCS network, Patni had a real-time picture of the jets in the air manoeuvring, targeting, locking on and launching.

There was no time to lose.

He ordered the primary long-range air search radar of his S-400 system to open up. Almost immediately, Patni had a lock.

The S-400 was a relatively new acquisition. It had never been tested in battle in the subcontinent. Its capabilities existed on a piece of paper, claims made by its Russian manufacturer. Until the first missile blasted off; no one really knew what to expect.

The jet that Patni engaged was more than 200 km away. The IAF had never taken out an aerial target at that range. Very few countries had.

'On the first night,' Patni admits, 'we had butterflies in our stomachs because the system had not been combat tested but it was now in a live operation. There are a lot of safeties which have to be removed before we carry out any kind of live operation, just to avoid any kind of accident.'

Safety systems for sophisticated weapons systems like the S-400 include a suite of engineered mechanisms, procedures and protocols designed to prevent accidental launches.

One by one, Patni called for them to be removed. The S-400s missiles were now prepped. A single button push was all that it would take to fire a round, each missile costing upwards of a cool $1.5 million.

'Taking out all the safeties was my call. Okay, remove this safety, remove that safety and so on. The final call that I gave was, "We are ready, the target has been assigned to us, we are ready to launch, the target is in the kill zone now, we can shoot it down."'

Patni took a deep breath. It was now or never. Would the system, a maze of high-tech engineering, actually work? Had he followed all his launch protocols? Was there any step that he had missed?

'The command [of the unit] is mine. However, the person who was pressing the button [to launch the S-400's missiles], was my number two, a Wing Commander.'

'I took a deep breath before giving my final call – "Okay, launch", and then it was the turn of my 2IC [second-in-command]. He asked me to confirm launch because this was the first time we had ever launched a surface-to-air missile into enemy airspace. We were trying to shoot down the enemy over his own territory.'

The Wing Commander set to depress the launch. He needed to know – one last time – if he had heard the orders properly.

'He asked me to confirm once again. "Sir, confirm fire." "Affirm," I said, "you are cleared to launch." It all took a couple of seconds, and then the missile was on its way.'

Time seemed to melt at that moment; it all seemed to be a haze. 'It felt like an eternity,' says Patni. 'The button had been pressed – was there something wrong?'

He then heard the boom. The earth shook under his feet as the missile – 25 feet tall – soared onto the night sky.

The S-400's missile accelerated to speeds well above Mach 5. The pilot who had been attacked now had seconds to attempt to out-manoeuvre the killer headed his way. His radar warning receiver would have been screeching an alert. He may have been dropping chaff and flares – decoys – in an attempt to deceive the incoming missile. Except, it didn't work.

'It's a huge sound and it actually lit up the entire sky, and after that sound, I heard one more sound. And that was the call of "Bharat Mata ki Jai". The men all started shouting "Bharat Mata ki Jai" after seeing that missile launch and everybody was charged up.'

Seconds later – 'Splash.' Patni laconically made the universal Air Force call-out announcing a successful hit.

The Pakistani fighter had been shot down. Its radar track disappeared off the screens of the S-400's radar and weapons controllers. 'We were hoping like hell that it could have been a J-10 so as to give him an even bigger slap, if possible,' he says with a smile. After systematic verification, the IAF chose to share that the fighter Patni shot down was a Chinese-built JF-17 'Thunder'.

It wasn't just Patni and his Wing Commander who had held their breath as the first S-400 was fired. While crews test extensively on simulators, nothing really prepared most at Adampur base for what happened when the system launched a live round. 'When the first S-400 was fired, my guys did not even know what had happened,' said Group Captain A.G. Kumar, the COO of the base. 'The sound of the missile launch was so loud that some of them thought a bomb had been dropped on them[.] I was very lucky to witness it firsthand,' he says, knowing he saw history being made in front of his eyes.

'Have you seen videos of Saturn 5 and Apollo 11 rockets being launched? It was actually like that. My son studies somewhere close to Phagwara. The students in this university could see missiles flying over their heads, intercepting incoming enemy missiles, with explosions in the sky. He sent videos back to us and asked, "Dad, are we at war?"'

Kumar laughs grimly. 'And I thought, "Well, you know about it now!" For them, it was akin to those Iron Dome missiles over Tel Aviv.'

Patni too, like Kumar, realised he had been part of something important. Adrenalin coursed through his body. 'I felt elated,' he says, looking back on that moment. 'I was raring to go. Okay, one after another. Let's get another one, let's get another one!'

The PAF backed off from the fight after recognising the threat. The IAF was now firing at them. Warnings of the S-400 launch would have been passed across PAF formations through radio alerts. With missiles that could reach 400 km, the Indian system could take them out deep within their own airspace. 'When they realised that we had started shooting back at them, they withdrew from the fight.'

With all their aircraft within the range parameters of the S-400, the PAF decided to live to fight another day. Their fighter formations went on the defensive and were barely seen in offensive formations till the ceasefire came into effect.

'Because of their defensive manoeuvring, they started going further westwards. My objective was achieved. In addition to wrecking destruction on the enemy, I could keep my fighters safe that was a part of my objective.'

When the controller's voice crackled through – target destroyed – the Node Commander did not react. 'It was just like going through a procedure, just like a surgeon,' he said later. 'Even when the strike against Bahawalpur was going through and "weapon released" was announced, there was no real sense of jubilation. You're not cheering, because the next thing on your mind is that you have to recover that aircraft. What will the enemy do now? I didn't have the time or the luxury to start getting happy or emotional. The next set of actions were already on the line.'

Phase One of the air battle was over.

This was the first time since 2019 that the IAF and PAF had fired in anger. Back then, following the IAF attack on Balakot, PAF fighters attempted to strike Indian Army targets in the Kashmir Valley. Wing Commander Abhinandan Varthaman, manning a Combat Air Patrol, scrambled in his MiG -21 to attempt an intercept of Pakistan Air Force fighters which had been detected operating in large numbers. Wing Commander Varthaman locked on to what the

IAF believes was a PAF F-16 . At the time, he faced at least four advanced PAF 4th gen fighters in that zone but refused to back down. In the melee that followed his aircraft was shot down. There is also clear-cut evidence on the basis of local accounts that another aircraft, a PAF fighter, also went down. Locals in the area saw two parachutes in the air. One belonged to Abhinandan who was captured. The other was of a PAF fighter pilot whose fate remains unclear. For his actions, Abhinandan became a national hero. He returned to India a few days later.

Six years later, the early hours of 7 May were something else: a massed, modern battle fought in the dark by two nuclear powers.

'The aim we set out with was hitting the terror infrastructure while avoiding escalation by not hitting the Pakistani Millitary,' Air Marshal Bharti said later. 'If we wanted to hit them, we would have started with their airfields and their air defence assets. As a nation we chose not to do that. That was really not the national intent anyway.'

He paused. 'If you see contemporary conflicts, they have been asymmetric air battles,' he added, pointing to Israel and the United States – wars where one side commanded the skies unchallenged. 'This was not that. Here was a situation where they also had a sizeable force, and we had a formidable force. It was a different kind of battle which has not happened in recent years.

By the time the first light crept over the horizon, the roar of engines had faded. Controllers logged their last radar returns, and the skies over the frontier were still again – except for the faint echo of what had unfolded above them.

6

It's War

7 May 2025–8 May 2025 (Morning)

After the initial air battle in the early hours of 7 May, the PAF withdrew and withheld the bulk of their fighters towards the west.

Instead, Pakistani forces almost immediately resorted to heavy cross-border artillery bombardment and small-arms fire targeting both civilian areas and military bases in northern and western India, with no intent of limiting collateral damage. Sectors of Jammu and Kashmir including Poonch, Rajouri, Kupwara, Baramulla and Akhnoor saw heavy shelling from Pakistan with the highest number of civilian casualties being reported on 7 May.

Foreign Secretary Vikram Misri would confirm the numbers on 8 May – 'Yesterday, Pakistan launched a targeted attack on the Sikh community of J&K, hitting a gurdwara in Poonch ... Three individuals were killed in the attacks ... A total of 16 civilians have been killed in Poonch and several others have been injured.'[15]

As night fell and darkness returned, Pakistan dramatically escalated by launching waves of drone and missile attacks against multiple military installations distributed across northern and western India, including Srinagar, Jammu, Pathankot, Amritsar, Ludhiana, Bathinda and Bhuj, forcing India's layered air defence network and counter-drone systems to engage targets.

'It was very clear that the Pakistani military had deliberately made itself a legitimate target for the Indian Armed Forces. So when they attempted to saturate us [with drones on the evening of 7 May and into the early hours of 8 May], we were prepared for it. They started sending in hordes of drones. We had to see where they were headed. We dealt with the intruding drones by analysing where they were headed, with the ones heading to civil population centres being accorded high priority. We used a combination of weapons [to engage the drones], in some cases surface-to-air missiles. In other cases, we used our close-in weapons systems – guns, hard-kill [missiles] and soft-kill options where you try and jam their frequencies. It was a layered defence which ensured that we did not have any damage,' said Air Marshal Bharti.

The tactical picture told its own story. Pakistan resorted to launching mass drone attacks into Indian territory, indiscriminately, hoping to detect any possible vulnerability in India's defences. This appeared to be an effort to glean intelligence by any means. This, ultimately, proved to be unsuccessful. The IAF and Indian Army were able to thwart these attacks – with drones either being shot down or rendered ineffective.

Alongside the drone attacks, the entire border region experienced intensified cross-border shelling and ground skirmishes. These were aimed at once terrorising Indian citizens along the Line of Control and international border. The Indian Army responded fiercely – with intense artillery shelling and missile strikes hitting Pakistani posts along the frontier with precision.

As Pakistan threw waves of drones at India's defences, the IAF chose its next step which was systematic destruction of the enemy's ability to fight back. The operations began during the night of 7 May and continued into the day of 8 May. The target: Pakistan's air defence architecture. The objective: hit radar installations and surface-to-air missile systems.

Understanding why these radars mattered requires a brief detour.

Pakistan's air surveillance network relied on two key radar systems of American origin: the AN/TPS-77 and the AN/TPS-43. The AN/TPS-77 represented a cutting-edge, mobile platform, enabling early warning at extended distances. In contrast, the AN/TPS-43 traced its lineage to the Cold War era, having entered US service in 1968. Despite its age, this robust system could track airborne targets up to 450 km away and had undergone multiple upgrades over the decades to maintain operational relevance. It now operated in tandem with modern Chinese YLC-6 radars, forming an integrated early-warning grid. Together, these systems served as the vigilant 'eyes' of the PAF, detecting incoming Indian aircraft from afar and facilitating timely intercepts.[16]

If the radars were the eyes of the Pakistan Army and Air Force, the Chinese-made HQ-9P, the customised variant operated by Pakistan since October 2021, was their powerful on-the-ground sword-arm. If the radars were the eyes of the Pakistan army and air force, the Chinese-made HQ-9P, the customised variant operated by Pakistan since October 2021, was their go to system. A long-range surface-to-air missile system, which the PAF was depending on. It was Pakistan's answer to India's S-400. The HQ-9P had an effective range of 125 km against aircraft, could track 100 targets simultaneously, engaging 8–10 of them at any one time. Pakistan had deployed these missiles around high-value sites like Rawalpindi, Karachi, Lahore and Sialkot. With Lahore just 50 km from the Wagah–Attari border crossing, it was especially dangerous.[17]

Neutralising any of these high-value assets would severely impair the adversary's operational capabilities. The weapon of choice for such precision strikes? Loitering munitions. Commonly referred to as suicide drones or kamikaze drones, loitering munitions mark a transformative evolution in modern warfare.[18]

Equipped with an explosive warhead, these unmanned systems are engineered to patrol a designated area – often for several hours – until a viable target is identified or manually selected. At that critical moment, they execute a terminal dive, colliding with the objective and detonating on impact, sacrificing themselves in the process.

The true ingenuity of loitering munitions lies in their adaptability. Unlike traditional missiles, which are irrevocably committed upon launch, these systems retain the ability to abort, loiter indefinitely or be reassigned to emerging threats. This makes them exceptionally effective against elusive targets – those that conceal themselves, surface only fleetingly or blend into the dense complexity of urban landscapes or rugged terrain.

The IAF, for its part, appears to have employed Israeli-designed Harop drones, footage of which appeared on social media.

Details on the Harop, available in the public domain describe it as being a fully autonomous loitering munition that seamlessly merges the speed and range of a missile with the endurance and surveillance prowess of a drone, delivering a potent and versatile strike platform.

On the morning of 8 May, the IAF demonstrated exactly how effective these weapons systems could be. The drone's sensors found what they were looking for – radar emissions from Pakistan's Chinese-origin HQ-16, a Pakistani surface-to-air missile unit in the Walton area of Lahore,[19] operated by its 4th Air Defence Regiment. These tell-tale signs were a signature, an electronic fingerprint impossible to hide. The moment the Pakistani crew activated their radar to scan for threats, they painted a target on themselves and became vulnerable to attack.

The weapon detonated its ordnance upon impact, destroying a mobile command post. A radar vehicle was also damaged in the attack, which injured four Pakistani soldiers.

Video of the attack emerged on social media, and it is mesmerising in its terrible precision. The footage shows a screaming loitering munition entering its terminal dive, a mechanical predator locked onto its prey. The drone's sensors having taken over, processed the data at electronic speeds, and made micro-corrections as it plummeted towards the target.

The strike carried significance beyond the immediate tactical damage. The HQ-16, system along with the longer-range HQ-9P, represented Pakistan's primary surface-to-air missile defence. Its destruction likely tore a significant gap in Islamabad's ability to defend airspace over one of its largest cities.[20] The air defence network that was trying to threaten IAF fighters just hours earlier was systematically destroyed by the IAF, proof of the IAF's capability to strike critical targets.

7

A Deadly 48 Hours

The events of 7 May from the late morning going into the night, however disruptive, were for the most part contained. But from the morning of 8 May, the Indian skies began to thunder.

The unmanned armada was a nightmarish mix: small commercial quadcopters that anyone could buy online possibly deployed to draw fire and deplete India's stocks of ammunition, military-grade reconnaissance drones meant to detect radar emissions and send back electronic intelligence about Indian sensors and imagery of defensive formations in real-time, loiter munitions such as the Turkish-manufactured YIHA-III and KaGeM suicide drones, designed to strike ground targets, and TB-2 Unmanned Combat Aerial Vehicles – heavily armed drones that had proven their lethality in conflicts from Libya to Nagorno-Karabakh. In the mix were also Fatah I and II rockets fired from multiple launch rocket systems and a handful of air-launched weapons.

Hundreds of drones crossed the LoC and the international border, penetrating Indian airspace. Small, cheap and expendable, their use in large numbers could have been potentially devastating. Pakistan was testing India's defences, searching for gaps, looking for vulnerabilities. They found none.

The IAF, meanwhile, continued to maintain robust air defence – fighters on combat air patrol, surface-to-air missile systems at full alert, radar networks scanning every cubic metre of airspace along the borders. They were ready for Round 2 of the aerial slugfest.

Three hundred drones were unprecedented: the Indian skies had never encountered drone attacks at this scale. But Pakistan was about to unleash something far worse – a storm of drones. These were launched indiscriminately, often with poor precision. They were unable to strike Indian military targets of any significance.

On the night of 8 May, blending into the early hours of 9 May, Pakistani forces intensified their drone attack. The activity spanned the entire front, from Kashmir to Gujarat, targeting military bases like

Srinagar, Avantipur, Jammu, Udhampur and Amritsar. As many as 600 drones – some armed, some for reconnaissance – were detected by the IAF that night.

Six hundred.

The IACCS nodes blazed with contacts lit up across the skies. From his underground node, the Node Commander watched the scenario develop. Even for a veteran with decades of experience reading the patterns of aerial warfare, the scale intrigued him.

'My reaction was, this is huge,' the Node Commander recalls. 'I didn't expect that they would come in such large numbers. Drones that were coming were being picked up well across the international border. They came in more in the Jammu and Kashmir sector than in our sector. [And they came in] a little bit in the central sector [of the area of operations of the Western Air Command].'

But one thing needs to be made absolutely clear, the Node Commander insists. Despite the fever-pitch rumours spreading across social media, despite the panic beginning to ripple through online forums and WhatsApp groups, the drones could never have threatened the capital.

The Node Commander categorically denies that drones came anywhere close to the NCR. 'Accounts on social media,' he says, 'are entirely incorrect. Nothing ever could come anywhere close to threatening Delhi. That I can tell you with authority and conviction. This was under my area of operations.'

Pakistan's expansive drone operations dipped on the morning of 9 May and then picked up with a vengeance that evening. 'On 9 May, once again, Pakistan's drone activity started around 8.30 p.m. We also assessed that there was a heavier buildup of aircraft and had inputs from Air Force channels of an imminent strike from their side,' says Air Marshal Bharti. The intelligence was clear. Pakistan was preparing something bigger. Along with the intense drone attacks, now came air-launched missile attacks from Pakistan's aircraft.

As on the 8 May night–9 May early morning, India saw attacks across IAF bases. The attacks themselves weren't particularly deep penetrations. These were assessed as relatively shallow strikes across the LoC and the international border, primarily targeting IAF bases and some Indian Army positions. But the scale was another matter.

The Pakistani strategy was transparent: saturate Indian air defences, force them to reveal their positions by firing, then localise and target Indian radars and surface-to-air missile systems. At the heart of battle, there lies a paradox: the minute you attack, you also reveal yourself and thus open yourself to attack. It was death by a thousand cuts, an attempt to overwhelm through sheer numbers. These were missions where the PAF appeared clearly unwilling to deploy its fighter aircraft.

India hit back. One senior officer noted, 'Once again, we responded by hitting their radar sites and surface-to-air missile sites in a bid to shape the battlefield.' The phrase 'shape the battlefield' is military speak for something more direct – degrading the PAF's ability to continue fighting as a formidable adversary, in this case, by targeting Pakistani Air Defence sensors, and progressively blinding them. This was a key objective woven into every strike mission.

'We needed to create some gaps by knocking off some of their sensors, some of their systems, so that we faced less and less resistance in our areas of interest and had the required degree of control of the air,' says Air Marshal Bharti.

The specific radars targeted by the IAF in this phase revealed just how deeply IAF planners understood Pakistan's air defence network. IAF strikes – both from the ground and air – reportedly destroyed three AN/

TPS-77 units at bases in Pasrur, Sialkot and Rahim Yar Khan. The destruction of these systems would definitely have severely degraded the PAF's radar network, creating blind spots through which Indian aircraft could operate with a higher degree of lethality.

The PAF aircraft, however, did not move in to engage the IAF's fighters. 'They were there but at further ranges,' says Air Marshal Bharti. They were playing defence, staying alive, preserving their combat power for a fight that might come later – or might never come at all.

In the meantime, back home, it was up to the IACCS nodes to manage the infernal chaos of the drone attack. The challenge was as much economic as tactical. Each drone that appeared on their screens demanded a decision: engage or ignore?

The calculus was brutal. A surface-to-air missile can cost millions of dollars and cannot be easily replenished – certainly not during an ongoing conflict. Some of the commercial drones the Pakistanis were using cost only a few hundred dollars. Shooting a million-dollar missile at a 300-dollar drone is the definition of an unsustainable exchange rate.

'Identifying everything in the air was the job of the node,' one officer explains. 'So, whatever I cleared to fly was a particular colour. Something which I had not identified as yet, was shown differently. Anything that I identified as a hostile, had another particular colour . . . Anything other than that was cleared to be engaged.'

This colour-coding system became the language through which critical decisions were made at machine speeds.

Drones have redefined military conflict around the world since the start of the Ukraine–Russia war. The footage from Ukraine's battlefields – first-person views from drones diving into Russian tanks, dropping grenades through tank hatches, hunting soldiers through forests and trenches – had made it clear. Unmanned systems weren't the future of warfare. They were the present.

At the time of Operation Sindoor, it is believed that the IAF already had procedures in place to counter mass-drone attacks. 'There are situations where we do practise for a saturation strike. Not just for drones. This was a saturation strike. So, there are procedures defined about how to tackle it. And we just followed that,' says the IACCS Node Commander.

While the S-400 system was instrumental in hitting high-value targets and fighter jets, shorter-range missiles deployed across the region took on the incoming drones. This included shoulder-fired surface-to-air missiles – several launched from frontline army posts, including high-altitude positions in Rajouri and Poonch, deployed mere metres from the LoC. Upgraded, radar-guided L-70 guns of the Indian Army were ordered to open fire on any drones they detected.

Other short-range and medium-range weapons the IAF used were MR-SAM, Akash, SpyDer, Pechora and SAMAR. The Army units were linked to a fully automated Air Defence Control and Reporting System (ADCRS) called the Akashteer ('sky-arrow' in Hindi), operating under the command and control of the IACCS.

One of the biggest challenges for each node commander involved in Operation Sindoor was ensuring that airborne targets designated for destruction were military, not civilian flights. This wasn't paranoia. This was based on hard evidence of what Pakistan was doing.

As tensions between India and Pakistan built up, even after India's strikes on multiple terror targets in Pakistan on 7 May, civilian airspace remained open over Pakistani airports. This was clear evidence of the PAF using civilian aircraft as shields for their fighters.

The goal? Confuse the air picture. Distract IAF surface-to-air missile batteries from launching, in the fear that innocent civilian flights would be hit. It appears hundreds of passengers ended up being used as human shields as PAF fighters manoeuvred near them and launched missiles at IAF targets.

'The really unscrupulous actions by our adversaries were that at a particular stage, they closed airspace in the lower half [of Pakistan] and diverted all their civil traffic to the northern part. Within that, they threw in their fighters. They funnelled in their civilian traffic to an area which would have hampered the operation of the S-400. There were very clear instances when we could make out that the [PAF] fighter is under the shadow of a civilian plane, perhaps without the civilian aircraft coming to know about it. Some aircraft would have gotten airborne from Lahore, others from Chaklala, Islamabad. You could make out [on the IACCS displays] that a projectile was coming from a civilian aircraft,' says the Node Commander.

The implications are staggering. Pakistani fighter pilots, operating under orders, were deliberately positioning themselves in the radar shadow of commercial airliners – planes filled with families, business travellers, students – using them as cover to launch attacks on Indian military targets.

It was a gambit that relied on Indian restraint. If the IAF fired and hit a civilian airliner by mistake, Pakistan would have an international incident of catastrophic proportions. Images of civilian wreckage and bodies would flood global media. India would be painted as reckless, trigger-happy, a danger to international aviation.

The Indian commanders held their fire when civilian aircraft were in the picture. They waited. They tracked. They let some shots go untaken rather than risk innocent lives. It was the right call.

As 9 May turned into the 10th, as drones swarmed the air and Pakistani fighters hid behind civilian airliners, the nature of this conflict fully revealed itself. This wasn't just a military confrontation. It was a test of systems, of doctrine, of national will – and of the moral lines nations would or wouldn't cross in pursuit of victory.

8

They Came for Adampur

8 May 2025 and on

Something else came along with the drones. Something much more destructive. From JF-17 fighters operating within the safety of Pakistani airspace, the PAF launched their CM-400 supersonic missiles, their response to India's BrahMos, India's most powerful air-to-surface missile. Their target: the S-400 air defence complex at Adampur Airbase.

The PAF realised that the S-400 that had brought down their plane on 7 May was the critical system that gave the IAF an edge. Without the defensive shield of these missiles, the IAF would not be able to operate as freely.

India had its operational S-400 regiments, strategically deployed to cover high-threat areas: around Punjab, western desert, China and wherever the threat matrix was highest. The PAF decided to focus primarily on Adampur. From the night of 7 May onwards, its mission was thus clear: take out the S-400 using the CM-400.

The CM-400AKG missile represented a potential game-changer for the PAF – if used successfully. These were high-speed Chinese weapons specifically designed to kill high-value targets – radar installations, command and control centres, the very infrastructure that allowed India to see and respond to threats.[21]

First unveiled at the 2012 Zhuhai Airshow by the China Aerospace Science and Industry Corporation, the CM-400AKG was an export-oriented system cleared for release to the PAF and integrated onto its fleet of Chinese JF-17 Thunder fighter jets. Operation Sindoor marked the first time this Chinese-developed supersonic air-to-surface weapon had been fired in anger.

The specifications read like something from a techno-thriller. The CM-400 missile flies at near-hypersonic speeds, reaching Mach 4–5 with a range exceeding 240 km, it does so while carrying a 150–200 kg warhead. In compression, although the larger BrahMos missile has top speeds of Mach 2.8–3.5 it carries a larger warhead of between 200–300 kg and has larger ranges. The missile integrates inertial navigation and GNSS (global navigation satellite system) guidance with a passive radar seeker for terminal precision. No wonder the Chinese marketed it as a 'carrier killer' if deployed against naval targets.

It wasn't just the CM-400. Between 8 and 10 May, Pakistani forces targeted Adampur with everything they had – drones, loiter munitions, air-launched weapons. If even one of these missiles found its mark, it could blind India's most advanced air defence system at a critical moment.

Adampur isn't just any airbase. Located approximately 20 km northeast of Jalandhar in Punjab, it's a lynchpin of the IAF's Western Air Command. A strategic forward base, it is one of India's most important air stations. Given its proximity to the border, it's designed for quick-response missions. Fighter squadrons based here are often first responders when enemy air threats are detected.

The base has a long history. Established as No. 305 Wing on 16 March 1950, Adampur was the launching point for some of the IAF's best-known missions during the Indo-Pak wars. In the 1965 war, vigilant defences thwarted PAF strikes, including a Pakistani Special Services Group commando drop on 7 September 1965, where 135 paratroopers were captured with assistance from locals. In the 1971 war, fighter interceptors from Adampur flew over 100 sorties, shielding Pathankot without a single successful PAF raid. During the 1999 Kargil conflict, French-built Mirage 2000 fighters from the base dropped guided bombs atop Tololing and Tiger Hill, paving the way for Indian soldiers to capture the heights.

The Pakistani attack on the first day of Operation Sindoor was defused by a missile launched from this base by Group Captain Animesh Patni and the team under his command. From 8 May on – and in particular through the nights of 8 and 9 May – Patni, the triumphant hunter of 7 May, came under attack. Engaging fighter jets was one thing, intercepting incoming cruise missiles was something else. This was the battle that Patni and the men under his command waged successfully through Operation Sindoor. By the end of active operations, Pakistani forces were unable to achieve a single hit on any S-400 units deployed in the conflict.

'Generally what we notice during peacetime are fighter aircraft. This was the first time I could see such a high-speed target coming up on my radar picture,' he says with feeling, the memory of those nights still vivid.

The incoming CM-400s were flying just short of a whopping Mach 5, significantly faster than India's own BrahMos. 'Initially [the speed of the CM-400] was a surprise for us. It was very fast. We had just a few seconds to [identify] the nature of the incoming threat. But the system performed absolutely in a fantastic way and exactly the way the Russians designed it [to function].'

Successfully neutralising an incoming high-speed land-attack missile, using a surface-to-air missile, is often likened to the immensely difficult feat of 'hitting a bullet with a bullet'. This analogy captures the sheer precision, extreme speeds and inherent operational complexity of such an engagement. It is one that the IAF's surface-to-air missile the squadrons train for. Given the velocities involved, there's no margin for even the tiniest error.

Publicly available analysis of the S-400 system indicates that it operates at least three different missiles, each designed to fly out to specific ranges. The missile speeds range from Mach 4 to Mach 14. With the incoming aggressor missile also supersonic, the closing rate drastically shrinks the window for interception, demanding pinpoint accuracy within severe time constraints. To make interceptions even more challenging, the CM-400 missiles launched by PAF jets are relatively small and likely manoeuvrable in their terminal phase.

After India's initial strikes, Group Captain Kumar and his team at Adampur had braced for the Pakistani response. The PAF attempted to overwhelm Indian Defences by saturating air defence systems –

launching a barrage of drones while simultaneously approaching the border, with the intent of pushing through missile attacks when the IAF's air defences were fully engaged. However, realistic training, constant drills, and the hands-on expertise of IAF air defence personnel and system operators ensured that what could have been a difficult day was effectively handled. Kumar and his team could track Pakistani aircraft flying even 300 km inside the Pakistani side of the international border. The missiles they were sending were at 'near hypersonic' velocity.

'I have seen close to 50 to 60 tracks with speeds bordering from 4,000 to 6,000 km per hour,' with a glint in his eyes, Kumar recalled adrenalin rush during the initial phase. 'They were moving towards us.'

Getting through that first night was extremely challenging putting him in a hyper alert and excited state. It was intense and the Pakistani CM-400 missile attack was an experience that tested training and character of this seasoned soldier. 'That night was a different kind of night. We were seeing the [missile or drone] track and then [it was] gone. Somebody has intercepted it. Another one coming and it's gone. One more intercepted. Some got through our defences – "Leak through, leak through!" – but then we engaged them with various short range systems at our disposal.'

'After that first night of the eighth, I got a call from Western Air Command. They were of the same opinion – that most of the missile tracks had been heading towards Adampur,' says Kumar.

Over those three days, Patni's radar screens lit up repeatedly with inbound threats – missiles with varying flight profiles, each one a puzzle to solve. There was one track that particularly unnerved him. 'We only saw the inbound missile,' he recalls. Which meant Patni had virtually no time to defend his unit and intercept the missile that homed in on him. 'We saw the inbound missile coming straight at us.'

Patni was not just defending IAF airspace, he was also striking back hard at every PAF asset that attempted to come against the IAF. There were also at least four other PAF fighters that he believes they brought down by 10 May. In each case these interceptions were either late at night or in the early hours of the morning.

The PAF's attempt to throw in the CM 400 did not succeed. But there were other threats closing in. Human ones.

While the PAF tracked Adampur from above – through radar networks and reconnaissance flights – people on the ground were hunting for the S-400's exact coordinates. The counterintelligence threat was serious enough to compromise the entire operation. 'It came as an eye-opener,' Patni says. 'We captured people and handed them over to civilian police. They were trying to give away our positions.'

Protecting the airbase from the PAF onslaught had made Patni's S-400 unit vulnerable. Their sensors had locked onto his radar signatures, feeding targeting data to missile crews across the border. Patni was aware the Pakistanis were hunting him. One of the advantages he had was the S-400 system was road-mobile.

One of the projectiles came close. It had evaded the first layer of IAF's air defences and was threatening to close in. It was engaged. 'We shot it down,' says Patni. 'This was a challenging case.'

What happened next was a pleasant surprise. Villagers in the area, who had seen the drone being taken out, cheered. 'Everybody was on their rooftops. For them, the launch of a missile was like *"Diwali ka pataka chal raha hai* [Diwali fireworks are going off]",' chuckles Patni, shaking his head. Villagers hailed Patni and his men as heroes, soldiers who had probably saved their village from being struck by the enemy.

The next morning, as the fighting abated, the

villagers came out to celebrate. They brought sweets, refreshments and homemade food for the battle-worn men. It was a touching moment for Patni and his team. They had not slept in days, and the pressure and need to focus was overwhelming. The unexpected hospitality and warmth around them gave them a brief respite.

'Even the Sarpanch, a lady, came and said, "Sir, *aapke liye humara pura gurudwara ka langar khula hai; aapko jab jo chahiye, khana chahiye, aap batayiye* [Sir, our gurudwara's kitchen is open to all of you; whenever you want, whatever you want, please tell us]." But Patni wouldn't be distracted. 'I sent one of my non-combatants over there to thank everyone.' He also sent the villagers gifts.

The moment was brief. The unit would need to move again. Now was not the time to celebrate. There was work to do, engaging targets when necessary.

On 10 May – just hours before the ceasefire – a CM-400 missile screamed into the Adampur Airbase. But it couldn't find its mark, detonating in an empty field. 'There was nothing actually there.' Open ground.

The same grit enabled him to turn the tables on his hunters next. Patni's radar operators were directed to spot something the IAF was trying to piece together from data from a host of radars deployed across the front.

Every night, the PAF deployed its fighter fleet, electronic warfare signatures – specifically efforts by PAF aircraft to jam Indian radars – bloomed on Indian screens. Somewhere out there, beyond what the Pakistanis believed was the S-400's outer engagement range, a high-value asset was orchestrating the aerial campaign – likely an AEW&C or a dedicated jamming platform. These force-multipliers were the PAF's central nervous system. Take one down, and you could break their will to fight.

'We were looking forward to an opportunity,' Patni says, 'to take down an HVAA – a high value aerial asset.' For Patni and his radar operators, triangulating that jamming source became an obsession. They tracked it night after night, running calculations, waiting for the perfect geometry of intercept.

'There were a lot of discussions to select the right parameters,' he recalls. 'The target was present on radar, but we needed to get our calculations right.'

Finally, on the last day of the war, all the dots had lined up and they chose their moment.

The same Wing Commander who'd fired the first S-400 missile on 7 May pressed the button again. Within seconds, the missile accelerated to optimal speed, tracking with algorithmic precision a target at the edge of possibility.

The Wing Commander's voice cut through the operations room: 'Standby for impact . . . standby for impact.' Then: 'Target destroyed. Destruction range: 314 km.'

For a moment, it didn't register. The S-400 had just intercepted an aircraft at nearly 200 miles – a range most observers considered theoretical at best. No system in its class had ever achieved this in combat.

Then one of Patni's team members broke the silence: 'Sir, this is supposed to be the longest-range one.'

The previous record had been set during the Russia–Ukraine war, where Russian forces operated the same system.

'That is an interception range even the Russians have not achieved so far,' Kumar says with quiet awe of the hit. 'That was a world record.'

The shootdown was of the single large aircraft – either an AEW&C aircraft such as the Swedish-built SAAB Erieye or an ELINT (electronic intelligence) aircraft, possibly a French-built Dassault DA-20, a specialised platform in use with the PAF since the eighties. It was a prize catch, clearly one of the most significant IAF achievements during Operation Sindoor. It was also the last Pakistani aircraft the IAF claims to have shot down during the 88 hours of active fighting between the forces of both sides.

For his actions, Group Captain Animesh Patni has been conferred with a Vir Chakra.

Despite multiple claims by Pakistani commentators that the PAF knocked out S-400 radars, not a single credible satellite image has emerged to prove any such hit. This contrasts sharply with multiple high-resolution satellite images showing the impact of IAF strikes on Pakistani airbases. India has consistently rejected the Pakistani narrative widely shared by anonymous online handles. Later, on 13 May, three days after Pakistan came to the cease-fire table, Prime Minister Narendra Modi visited Air Force Station Adampur. He was filmed in front of an S-400 launcher. The message was clear: contrary to Pakistani claims, no S-400 unit had been struck.

'When things calmed down a bit on the tenth morning, we knew that we had done a fantastic job. They weren't able to get a single thing. Adampur didn't lose anything. The tactical brilliance of Western Air Command and the way they organised their offensive and defensive posture – the way they were deployed and employed on that night was like watching a Zubin Mehta orchestra. Despite their best efforts, they couldn't get through,' says Group Captain Kumar proudly.

What also gets forgotten is the fact that Adampur wasn't just a defensive fortress. It was also a frontline fighter base.

Upgraded MiG-29s screamed off the runway daily, flying combat air patrols to keep Pakistani fighters at bay. Indian MiGs continued to maintain station despite knowing that the math wasn't in their favour. Their Russian-built R-77 air-to-air missiles had decent range – but the PAF's new J-10 fighters carried PL-15s that comprehensively outranged the primary air-to-air missiles of the MiGs.

Kumar, an experienced fighter pilot himself, understood exactly what his men faced every time they climbed into those cockpits. 'When you see people go to war, you hope all of them come back.' His voice is measured, careful. 'Adampur had prepared well and the training and preparation bore rich dividends. We didn't lose a single man or machine. All of them came back.'

'That concern is always there – that someone doesn't come back and then you have to break the news, you have to look after the families.' He pauses, the weight of command sitting heavy in those words. 'At my level, you get used to it. You're mature enough to handle such situations. All this is part and parcel of operations. If you go into combat operations, you will suffer losses. Some people will not come back. You will lose machines.'

'Our youngsters do most of the fighting. Their emotions tend to be higher, so you need to keep that under control and ensure they concentrate.' He recalls his Air Officer Commanding addressing the entire station before the shooting started, 'Boys,' he said, 'they will try and hit us. And you have to keep at it even if there are bombs dropping next to you. That part – the emotions – have to be controlled.'

Then Kumar's voice shifts, thinking of the ingenuity, courage and dedication of each and every man at Adampur base. It carries something else now. Pride. Satisfaction earned through fire.

'This is a true report card of what you have been preparing to do all your life,' he says.

9

Danger at the Front

8 May 2025–9 May 2025

The PAF's aerial swarm came not just for the S-400 but for the bases around the LoC. Srinagar would face its most intense aerial assault in decades in those two days.

Somewhere ahead of Jammu, along the LoC in Jammu and Kashmir, Group Captain Gupta stood drenched in the sweltering heat, sweat soaked his head beneath the helmet, while the bulletproof vest chafed painfully against his skin, grinding raw rashes into his flesh. Yet his focus remained elsewhere. The unit under his command was deployed perilously close to the border at a time when relations between the two nations had reached their nadir. A deadly confrontation loomed as an inescapable reality – grim, tense, teetering on the brink of eruption. He occupied an elevated position, a vital vantage point that allowed him to survey a considerable distance in all directions. He needed that oversight. The area was riddled with Pakistan-sponsored terrorism – a classic counter-insurgency (CI) zone in army parlance. His primary duty was air defence: eyes fixed on the sky, monitoring radar screens for threats from above. Still, he frequently stole glances upward for another reason – he was well within range of enemy artillery. These dual threats explained the heavy bulletproof vest he wore despite the discomfort. In such an exposed spot, camouflage was equally critical. He had to remain still, silent and ever-watchful to fulfill his role effectively.

Gupta had been battle-ready, almost as soon as Pahalgam happened, moving his Akash surface-to-air missile unit. By the time his unit reached its final position, they had travelled significant distances from their base through a few state lines, finally to their location north of Jammu. Moving an Akash battery, with many vehicles with combat units travelling through day and night, was punishing work. On 7 May, he watched the air picture develop in the predawn darkness. He didn't know the full scope of what India had struck, but the feed from IACCS told him enough: he could be called into action at any moment.

That night, he was locked in a deadly calculation. Open his radars, and he could track and destroy enemy aircraft or drones. But those same radar emissions would betray his position, allowing Pakistani forces to triangulate his location and strike. Stay silent, stay hidden – yet remain blind, like a wild cat on a hunt in the dark, it was often an exceedingly difficult choice.

'We were monitoring the IACCS,' Gupta recalls. 'We were not disclosing our locations by opening radars; nobody does that. On IACCS, I could see the action, news had started flowing in so definitively – we saw a lot of action on his [the enemy's] side.'

So he waited. And watched.

His missile launchers and their associated radar and control vehicles sat under heavy camouflage, scattered across a designated area. Not only did Gupta have to monitor for air threats, he had to guard against something more immediate: terrorists attempting to infiltrate across the border.

'Ground security was a major concern to us,' Gupta explains. 'Though we were in an army area, the army was also moving. There was a lot of movement.' With Indian forces repositioning across the region, securing his dispersed Akash battery became his primary responsibility.

The Akash – Sanskrit and Hindi for 'sky' – is India's homegrown answer to aerial threats. Developed by the Defence Research and Development Organisation (DRDO) under the Integrated Guided Missile Development Programme that began in the eighties, it was designed to replace aging Russian systems that had formed the backbone of IAF air defence since the early sixties. The Soviet S-75 Dvina, acquired after the 1962 war with China, had become obsolete by the eighties. India needed something modern. Something indigenous.

Building the Akash required breakthrough innovations in ramjet-rocket propulsion and sophisticated radar integration. It was manufactured by Bharat Dynamics Limited and Bharat Electronics Limited, and supported by more than 200 smaller companies supplying components. The Air Force inducted it in 2014; the Army followed in 2015. Despite early teething problems – common with any new weapons system – Akash proved itself a formidable addition to India's air defences.

The system is mobile, mounted on wheeled or tracked transporter-erector-launchers that can relocate quickly to avoid detection. Each battery can reportedly track up to 64 targets while engaging 12 simultaneously. The missiles themselves accelerate to Mach 2.5, using a unique integrated ramjet-rocket engine that maintains high speed throughout flight unlike traditional systems that rely mainly on their initial booster phase. Weighing 720 kg, with a 60 kg pre-fragmented warhead, each missile can intercept targets up to 25–30 km out and altitudes up to 20 km.[22]

The nerve centre is the highly networked battery structure. A 3D central acquisition radar provides 360-degree surveillance, identifying threats. The Rajendra Radar, a 3D passive electronically scanned array, tracks targets, guides missiles and resists enemy jamming.

'It's a beautiful system,' Gupta says. 'We should proudly call it indigenous. Since this is our system, we can customise and make changes in it very fast.' Within days of the fighting winding down, technical experts from Bharat Electronics Limited visited his unit and implemented on-the-spot fixes to operational issues he'd identified. 'All our problems that need to be resolved are resolved easily.' Foreign systems, he noted pointedly, don't come with manufacturer support during a conflict. The Akash did.

In Srinagar, 300 km away, Group Captain Jijo Jose Ovelil also waited out 7 May. Little did he know that in the next 48 hours of 8 and 9 May, he would face the most challenging days of his career.

With 2,000 flying hours on MiG-21 Bisons, Sukhoi-30 MKIs and MiG-29UPGs – including carrier operations off INS *Vikramaditya* – Ovelil's first instinct when Operation Sindoor began was simple: he should be in a cockpit. But as COO at one of the IAF's most strategically vital bases, Ovelil had a different responsibility. He would run everything.

In 2019, during the Balakot strikes, Ovelil had been attached to a flying unit, on standby to scramble. 'By the time I reached my base, where I was attached for flying, the entire thing was over.' Six years later, in Operation Sindoor he would experience war firsthand. What happened next, required him to bring in the training he received at the NDA and the IAF and the invaluable experience gained through years of operations and flying.

'I've spent 24 years in the Air Force, but this was my first operation,' he says. 'There was relief, because everyone was waiting for something to happen. There was excitement that it was finally starting.'

But Srinagar AF Station wasn't just runways and hangars. It was a mini-township – home to thousands of military families who would need protection when Pakistan responded to India's 7 May strikes on the nine terror targets.

'The easiest part was telling my men and women to be ready. That's what we train for, what we prepare for. Since we knew something was coming, we were in place,' Ovelil explained. 'The trickier part was briefing the families, who also live here. We had everything in place. We had trenches and shelters earmarked. Informing children and families that in case of an air raid warning, they needed to get into trenches or shelters. That was tricky. For the children, it was exciting – they had fun. But there was anxiety among the families, though their support was phenomenal. During Operation Sindoor, everyone was doing their job, working 24/7. Some people you'd normally hear complaints from were fully committed! No one asked, "Sir, I need to go somewhere."'

Srinagar Air Force Station's operational history reads like the IAF's greatest hits: the 1947 airlift that saved Kashmir, Flying Officer Nirmal Jit Singh Sekhon's posthumous Param Vir Chakra in 1971 for taking on six Pakistani F-86 Sabres alone, the 1999 Kargil operations and the 2019 Balakot strikes when Wing Commander Abhinandan Varthaman engaged a Pakistan Air Force F-16. Operation Sindoor would add another chapter.

On 7 May, Ovelil, like Gupta, watched the screen intently, monitoring his sector while maintaining a connection to the broader air battle. 'I didn't have the larger picture as to what was happening, but we could see aircraft getting airborne across [the border] and we were thereafter concentrating only on the targets that were allotted to us. On the first day, there was not much that I could see. We were given threats but most of them were being tackled before they came anywhere near us on the first day.'

Then 8 May arrived. For 48 hours through 9 May, India's air defences faced their greatest test since 1971. Nine hundred aerial threats. Constant artillery. Fighter squadrons on hair-trigger alert. Most of the action was focused on Indian Army positions just across the LoC and the international border.

At Gupta's position, the Jammu region, the Akash units became critical players in India's defence. His unit was part of an integrated network of multiple Akash batteries protecting dozens of square kilometres. Hundreds of highly trained IAF personnel manned these positions, networked together for coordinated launches.

The system proved its worth on 8 and 9 May, when Pakistani drone attacks intensified across the sector. There were moments when they tracked enemy drones, achieved lock and came within seconds of firing. The Akash batteries provided crucial deterrence during these waves of drone incursions – though actual launches weren't always necessary, largely because IAF jamming systems confused the incoming drones' navigation and control systems, causing them to drop harmlessly when they ran out of fuel.

Jamming, among the IAF's most closely guarded secrets, played a major role in the success of Operation Sindoor. Radio frequency jammers emit powerful electromagnetic waves on the same frequencies drones use for communication and navigation, overwhelming or blocking their signals. When jammed, drones lose contact with their operators. Depending on their programming and the jamming intensity, they hover, attempt to return home or simply drop from the sky. India deploys DRDO's D4 (Drone-Detect, Deter and Destroy) anti-drone system which combines RF jammers with radar and electro-optical sensors, along with portable rifle-style jammers for short-range defence.[23]

At Srinagar, air defence systems sprung into action.

'Against most of them, we launched weapons,' Ovelil said. 'We had certain protocols in place, based on the kind of target, the speed that it had and the type of weapon which would take it out – right from the counter-air system till the long-range vectors. Everything was used, including the guns. We were handed targets by the nodes that we have and their battle manager controlled it from there and our weapon control was handed to us.'

The threat picture was murky. Were they facing fighter jets? Advanced drones? 'It is difficult to say whether we detected fighter aircraft – that's something that's based on the radar cross section (RCS) and the speed of the aircraft. There were some fast movers but you can't be sure whether there were fighter aircraft or whether there were UCAVs [unmanned combat aerial vehicles] or something else, because the speeds of UCAVs were also pretty high. So we are not sure what it was but there were certain targets that were detected, and based on that, we utilised our systems.'

Across Srinagar, residents heard air defence guns open fire. Drones appeared in the sky. Surface-to-air missiles occasionally streaked upward, leaving plumes. It was terrifying – and it was about to get worse.

By 9 May, the assault intensified dramatically. Air Marshal Bharti's intelligence assessment was proving accurate: Pakistan was building towards something bigger.

The rules of engagement had changed. This was no longer about deterrence. This was about survival.

'Between the ninth and the tenth was the time

when we had the maximum number of aerial vehicles – UCAVs, drones and everything else,' Ovelil recalls. 'We had air defence in place. Like we have a lot of counter-unmanned systems as well. Everything was in place. So we were able to deter or neutralise most of the threats before they came anywhere near to where they could have caused damage.'

Every decision carried weight. Activate radars and you could track and destroy threats – but you'd also reveal your position. Stay quiet and you might miss the kill shot. It was a deadly calculus repeated hundreds of times across those 48 hours.

Ovelil had moved his bed into his office. 'I think in those four days I would have slept for barely a few hours in total. We had the other officers in place but every time we used to have a break and would try and go and sleep, somebody would be waking me up again and back at it. So, in those 96 hours, I think I must have slept for about four hours.'

The spirit around him was indomitable. 'The josh was tremendous. There were non-combatants who were tremendously aware and ready. We had our non-combatants serving tea during an air raid with the lights out, cycling and going by vehicles with the lights out. Just because they knew that there are people at all kinds of places waiting and they are there throughout the night, throughout the day. There were air warriors who were willing to stay and sleep at the base and anytime the air raid came on they were already at their post even though it was not their duty. Just so that in case there is something wrong, the people were already ready to take on tasks. People were actually asking, "Is there anything more I can do, is there anything else I can contribute?" because once their tasks were over, people were again calling up and asking, "Can I do something more? Can I do something to help?" I'm really proud to have been there at that point of time. I got help in the sense everybody was doing their job; they were going beyond their charter, actually. I don't have any other words [with which] I can describe it.'

Maintenance crews worked miracles. Fighter jets require hours of ground-work for every hour in the air. With war on, serviceable aircraft meant survival.

'We had equipment being prepared in record time because everybody was there and working 24/7. In the build-up to 7 May, maintenance was actually working overtime. With all the equipment that we had at base, aircraft, surface-to-air guided weapons, they were all working overtime. And they actually managed to get us into a very, very healthy state,' Ovelil says. 'Something which during peacetime we don't normally see, because everything has a certain cycle, everything has a certain time frame. But during operations, it was phenomenal the way they were working. They worked overtime, they got everything in order, they got things rectified very, very fast.'

Even weather couldn't stop them. 'In between, it rained as well. At times, water affects equipment. They were, again, really, on it. We had things back [in action] in just an hour or so,' Ovelil notes. 'We did not have any kind of unsustainability that lasted for more than maybe half an hour or so.'

One maintenance officer called, asking if he could help with base defence or drone spotting after finishing his primary duties.

At Srinagar, the training paid off. Despite the drone assault and munitions launched over 8 and 9 May, despite the artillery strikes, despite the sustained aerial assault – Srinagar AF Station suffered no damage.

But for Ovelil, the fighter pilot's instinct never left. 'My first thought was I should have been flying. That was my first thought. But then, this is also an important job,' he says with a smile.

Once the action started, there was no time for

reflection. 'Training kicked in. There was not much time to even think. We were doing things like clockwork. Getting something allotted, passing it on, next target, passing it on, checking if everything is in order . . . And the time we had in between, we were trying to sleep or have food. That was actually the way it was going, so there was nothing much beyond that. Yes, there was this pride that finally we are doing something that we have trained for.'

Being minutes from the LoC meant Pakistani radars tracked every IAF fighter the moment it took off. Every sortie carried mortal risk.

'There is a sort of a rollercoaster of emotions. When you launch aircraft, they're offensive, they're supposed to be doing their job, but you also want them to land back. I mean, Srinagar being so close to the LoC – there was always anxiety and this happened every time. I was caught in a cycle of emotions. You're excited and they get airborne and you're looking forward to the battle and then there's anxiety and worry. They land back. Then there's relief. But by the time the relief can set in, you are already preparing for the next thing.'

Through it all, there was no major hit by an incoming missile or drone on any significant target in Srinagar. Akash and MR-SAM batteries stood ready, their radars sweeping the sky, their missiles primed. The jammers disrupted hundreds of drones. The maintenance crews kept every system operational. The families sheltered in trenches, while their loved ones manned the guns.

It was a testament to training, indigenous air defence systems, jamming technology and, above all, the men and women who refused to break under the most intense pressure they'd ever faced.

As day broke on 10 May, it was clear that the siege had been defeated. Virtually none of the IAF's assets had been harmed – missile units, planes, bases, runways were untouched. But the country's sleepless soldiers, ever on alert, knew that the story hadn't ended.

10

The Final Day

10 May 2025

The crew room fell silent when Group Captain Ranjeet Singh Sidhu walked through the door shortly after midnight on 9 May 2025. A bunch of pilots sat on standby, ready to scramble at a moment's notice. They'd been flying combat missions for three days straight. They were wired. And when their Commanding Officer spoke, they knew exactly what was coming.

'I just entered the room and said, "Boys, the time has come – let's go again."'

Every pilot in the room stood up.

'They were all pumped up and they – all of them – stood up [each one getting set to go]. So I had to pick and choose from them who would go. [I told the others], "Don't worry, it will continue."'

Sidhu quickly kit up. They had to move. Now. With each consecutive strike, the IAF had been raising the level of its assault – hitting harder with more firepower at bigger targets. This mission would push even deeper into Pakistani airspace.

His pre-flight ritual had become familiar over the

past three days. 'I walked to the aircraft. I met my men who had prepared the aircraft and exchanged a few words with them. And I told them, "All of you are going to be a part of history," I went around my aircraft, checked its readiness. I also kissed my weapon.'

Around him, the ground crew radiated intensity. 'I then climbed up the ladder and you could see the body language of all the men working under me. It was very positive.'

The Rafales had a secure internal network, invisible to the outside world. 'We don't give a radio transmission to the outside world [when an operation is live]. "Okay, let's start up." So we started up. Even the responses that I was getting [from the other pilots] indicated that they were all charged up.'

Station authorities had gathered on the tarmac – officers, the station commander, the Air Officer Commanding standing next to Sidhu's aircraft as engines spooled up. 'All gave me thumbs up. And with that, carrying those hopes and a sense of responsibility, we taxied out.'

Hours before the ceasefire that would end the fighting, Sidhu's Rafale formation was going back into war.

The decision to escalate had come past midnight, in the early hours of the morning on 10 May. Pakistan's escalation over the previous 24 hours – hundreds of drones, Fatah rockets, CM-400 hypersonic missiles screaming toward Indian military targets – demanded a response that would rewrite the rules of engagement.

What had begun on 7 May as strikes against terrorist targets was about to become something even larger. Operation Sindoor was no longer just about hitting terror camps – this was now a full-on assault on the heart of the PAF, its pride and joy: its airbases.

The IAF was now poised to hit radars, infrastructure, surface-to-air missile units, runways, hangars, dispersal areas and command and control centres. The IAF says these were proportionate responses – in fact, they were massive.

But even as the IAF prepared to retaliate, the strategic calculus remained clear. This was a graded response – deliberate, methodical, calibrated to send a message without crossing into total war.

The strikes would prove the point: 'Our response has always been graded – to drive home a message to the adversary – that if you want to escalate, we are more than willing to match-up and give you a befitting reply. The targets were also chosen accordingly. It was a graded response, we could have gone in a much bigger way.'

Between 2.00 a.m. and 5.00 a.m. of 10 May, IAF strike packages lit up the night sky across Pakistan. One after another, precision weapons found their marks. The targets weren't hidden terror camps anymore. These were the crown jewels of Pakistani military aviation.

Chaklala. Rahawali. Rafiquy. Rahim Yar Khan. Sukkur. Murid. Nayachor.

All key PAF bases. High-resolution satellite imagery broadcast first on NDTV would later confirm what the IAF pilots already knew: they had hit hard, they had hit clean and they weren't done.*

The attacks did not end then. The IAF resumed attacks, five hours later, at 10 a.m. In the next two hours, Sargodha, Bholari and Jacobabad were hit. The airfields were attacked 'mostly by long-range, standoff weapons. While this was happening, we were also hitting their radars and surface-to-air missile sites which were done by a combination – mainly by our loiter munitions,' said Air Marshal Bharti.

Pakistan, for its part, continued trying to target India during the same time period. 'They were firing

____

*Detailed description of IAF hits on Pakistan Airbases detailed with satellite imagery of the hits in the Appendix.

Fatah rockets at us, loiter munitions. They also targeted us by firing the CM-400 missile. We intercepted the CM-400, we jammed them, while some of them fell on open ground.'

There was constant danger in carrying out the strikes. Connected with other jets in his formation through a data-link and flying under the watch of both ground controllers and an IAF AWACS aircraft, Sidhu was aware he was being actively targeted.

'I could see adversary aircraft [on my radar] across [the boundary] but they couldn't do anything about our strikes.'

They were trying, though. Pakistani fighters manoeuvred desperately. Ground-based radars painted Sidhu's jet, feeding targeting data to surface-to-air missile batteries, attempting to lock on his jet and launch against him. Lock-on warnings screamed in cockpits.

But Sidhu had one huge advantage: SPECTRA – arguably the world's most advanced electronic warfare suite.

The SPECTRA (Système de Protection et d'Évitement des Conduites de Tir du Rafale) is the integrated electronic warfare suite of the Dassault Rafale fighter. It provides comprehensive 360-degree self-protection by combining detection and countermeasure functions. Using multispectral sensors (radar, laser and missile-approach warners) and high-speed processors, SPECTRA automatically detects, classifies and counters threats in real time without pilot input. Its signature capability is active cancellation, which involves emitting counter-phase signals to effectively 'erase' the Rafale from enemy radars.[24]

'SPECTRA is one of the world's most advanced electronic warning suites. It ended up being a huge advantage, Pakistani radars and missiles tried to lock onto Rafales, but SPECTRA defeated them repeatedly. Yes, the adversary fired a lot of missiles but they were defeated successfully,' Sidhu says. '[It] was giving us indications [of inbound Pakistani missiles].'

For pilots in the Rafale formations, SPECTRA ended up being a fundamental gamechanger, a cutting-edge defensive shield that protected pilots and the jets they were flying.

Alongside the Rafales flew the Sukhois armed with their supersonic BrahMos. Group Captain Manav Bhatia was leading one of those squadrons. His co-pilot sitting in the front of the plane was one of the youngest of his pilots, an enthusiastic 27-year-old fighter pilot.

They had already gone through what was expected in the sortie four times, both in the cockpit and before that in the briefing room. So when the operation was underway, things were happening automatically. 'There was beautiful synergy,' Bhatia says, between the two men.

'This was a mission without any radio calls. There were no external RT [radio transmission] calls which were given – not even one. It was dark. Every light that you saw from the west made you wonder, "Is that [an enemy] surface-to-air missile launch?" We were talking between the front and rear cockpits, me in the rear, my co-pilot up front. "What is that?" "No, it's nothing, it's a star."'

Bhatia had decided earlier that when the time would come to launch the missile, he would give his youngster a chance. He had had 20 years of service. Now he wanted to give the young man sitting along with him 'the kick of the trigger press'.

'I could see the confidence building up in him. The plan was working out.'

The long-range NO11M Bars radar on his Su-30 MKI was picking up tracks of PAF jets across the Indo-Pak boundary. There were dozens of jets in the air. The possibility of the enemy launching was very real. Equally real was the threat of being picked up by radars of Pakistan's Chinese-built HQ-9 missile system.

Bhatia's Radar Warning Receiver was picking up attempts by Pakistani radar to track his aircraft. 'Lock-on was there,' he says but he also knew they were relatively safe and outside lethal threat range.

'When we turned towards the final launch aspect, the last few seconds – that is the time I felt that all I needed to do was to fold my hands and say to myself, *ab kar lega yeh*. He will now manage.

I gave the call: "You are cleared for firing."

He said, "Ready to launch!"

I said, "Okay, launch."

And he said, "Pressing trigger . . ."'

All these months later, the feeling of launching the deadly BrahMos remains vivid to Bhatia. 'The BrahMos is a beautiful weapon when it leaves your aircraft. It's like a sunrise in the middle of the night.

When I was pressing the trigger, I prayed in my heart, *Bas, bulls eye mar de yarr, please* let the launch and hit be perfect.

And then – *gayi!* She's gone!

On the intercom I said, "Very nice."

And then that thing lights up on our head-up display screen (HUD) because it's the boost phase, and the youngster starts handling the aircraft like

Maverick in *Top Gun* – and we are now doing our post-launch manoeuvres.

The kinetic energy that the BrahMos stores is massive. [Over and above the size of its warhead], the high Mach velocity with which it hits its target – the kinetic energy is so massive that you cannot hide the damage. We hit critical enemy infrastructure,' Bhatia concludes proudly.

All strikes used precision standoff weapons fired from 300 to 600 km away, demonstrating the accuracy of India's new generation of missiles. They all deliberately targeted military assets while avoiding civilian areas.

The success of these strikes was validated through independent images procured by this author from Maxar (now Vantor), among the premier global suppliers of military-grade satellite imagery. Many of these images have been freshly labelled and reproduced in this book.

The damage done was immense – more details of which are in the appendix:

- **Sukkur, Sindh province**: A hangar completely collapsed, with twisted steel beams and debris scattered across the tarmac. This was believed to be a hangar for unmanned aerial vehicles.

- **PAF Base Nur Khan, Rawalpindi, Punjab province**: PAF Base Nur Khan is situated about 10 km southeast of Islamabad. This was the most symbolic strike, hitting Pakistan's drone operations centre just 10 km from the capital. Satellite imagery showed a major command-and-control facility was obliterated, far beyond the initial two vehicles reported destroyed. Pakistan's Prime Minister was awakened at 2.30 a.m. with news of this hit.

- **Rahim Yar Khan, southern Punjab**: A last-minute addition after intelligence suggested it would be used for offensive operations. A 13-m crater destroyed the runway centreline.

- **PAF Base Mushaf, Sargodha, Punjab:** Two massive craters severed the main runway, rendering it inoperable.

- **PAF Base Shahbaz, Jacobabad, northern Sindh**: India struck an F-16 maintenance hangar. The IAF states that four to five F-16s were destroyed inside, though the US State Department refused to comment on the status of Pakistan's American-made fighters, despite US contractors monitoring every F-16 in Pakistan's fleet.

- **Bholari Airbase, northern Thatta district, Sindh**: A precision strike, destroyed a hangar believed to contain a SAAB Erieye AWACS aircraft –

Pakistan's 'eyes in the sky'. The Chief Minister of Sindh confirmed 6 PAF personnel were killed.

While Rafales and Sukhois created devastation, Squadron Leader Gupta's Akash surface-to-air missile battery faced an inferno along the J&K front.

The early morning brought waves of saturation attacks. Pakistani drones and missiles filled the sky.

'Lot of weapons were falling on tenth morning. These weapons came around 5.40 a.m. There were some weapons which fell near our location where we were deployed around 200–300 m away from me. The ground beneath our feet shook, we immediately took cover. Everybody was flat on the ground, the shock wave knocking the air out of their lungs. Helping one another up, they gathered themselves and soon got back to work,' Gupta said.

None of his men had experienced this before. The proximity of the explosions – close enough to feel the shockwave, to taste the cordite – left no room for debate. They had to move.

Relocating under fire is among the most dangerous operations a missile battery can attempt. 'When we are moving, we are not in a state to fire. So the other system, which was [providing] an envelope over us, had fired at that point of time,' Gupta says.

Gupta's unit moved a few kms forward from their original position.

An Army officer found them at the new location with an unwelcome briefing, he said, 'Sir, why have you come here?' I asked him, 'Why? What wrong with this place?' He responded, 'Sir, there is a high likelihood of heavy shelling here.'

By around 10 a.m., as the Indian fighter jets were destroying more Pakistani bases, Gupta had deployed. He was in the middle of a tornado which seemed to have no end. For the first time he thought of death. He adapted his tactics, hoping for the best while preparing for the worst. 'I gathered all my men. We planned our strategy with only one-third of our strength, so that even if there was damage, it was minimised. We had our men with guns positioned in the periphery to have some security. And we were ready.'

His mood was grim but utterly focused.

Little did he know that far away from him, the war was reaching a turning point. Throughout the early hours of 10 May and into the morning of the same day, multiple videos emerged on social media, indicating massive explosions in several areas targeted by the IAF.

By the time Siddhu's Rafale touched down from that final mission, videos were already streaming across Indian television. 'As we landed, the videos were already out on television and it was as if the cricket World Cup final is underway and suddenly from our side somebody has hit the winning sixes.'

For Sidhu, the operation was especially important. He had spent 20 years in the IAF, flying fighters across different squadrons, finally ending up as a Commanding Officer of the IAF's newest and most lethal asset – a Rafale squadron.

As his tenure wound down, he made peace with the fact that he would never see combat. Twenty-five days. That's all that remained before Sidhu would hand over command. Then Pahalgam happened and Siddhu finally, finally got an opportunity to serve his motherland.

Within a few hours of the strikes, at about 3.30 p.m., word came that the Pakistani Director General of Military Operations – the same officer who had rebuffed his Indian Army counterpart three days earlier when the crisis began – called India to negotiate ceasefire terms.

When the request came, India had the edge. 'It's not that we were relieved. We were on a song. There was no way, with their present capability, that they could have stopped us. Yes, there could have been some damage on our side if the hostilities continued but that is what conflicts are about. We would have been able to hit whatever we wanted to hit,' says Air Marshal Bharti.

Even as the Sidhu taxied back to his shelter, more Rafales from his squadron were tasked to engage additional targets – in fact, at the time the ceasefire talks concluded, Rafales were airborne. Their targets remain classified.

'When the order to stand down came, a few of my aircraft were already in the air. And some of the aircrew were walking to the aircraft for the next [strikes to follow]. And if we hit those, then the world would have known. We were raising the levels with each strike. [But these jets] were called back,' Sidhu says.

The ceasefire would take effect at 5.30 p.m. on 10 May 2025 – bringing Operation Sindoor to a close after three days of sustained combat operations.

On the J&K frontline, Gupta couldn't believe the news that was being reported by the media. Then the order came through to stand down. 'News came that we have to stand down. That's when we realised that things are cooling off and that whatever we saw in the media was right.' Gupta's unit never fired a missile during Operation Sindoor. But those few days under constant threat – from drones, missiles, artillery and potential ground infiltration – became a crucible for his men.

When on his way back from an essential task with the units second-in-command, he saw a temple. As he headed to the temple to thank the gods for wisdom and strength to rise up to the occasion, he was interrupted, the war wasn't quite over on his front. 'The moment we went over there, the shelling started again. Again, we rushed back to our place. The shelling started on tenth night, probably till two or three o'clock in the night. After that it was over.' Finally, finally Gupta could rest easy.

He and his men had been thrown into the line of fire, desperately trying to stay clear of the barrage of drones, missiles, and artillery that came their way – ultimately relying on the training ingrained in him from the time he was a cadet aspiring to join the IAF. Every day that he had survived was a testament to his determination, optimism and passion. But it wasn't his alone.

Every single man and woman who fought for India shared those emotions – they couldn't have been more different, from battle-hardened veterans to

20-something pilots to the officers in the underground node who barely slept through those 88 hours. But they all felt the same emotions, their hearts kept the same beat.

Wars are fought using strategy at the highest levels and complex weaponry out of a sci-fi film, but they are won because of the determination and will of the men and women on the frontline.

That same attitude permeated across every level of the IAF. Group Captain Kalra had an unexpected exchange after his Sukhoi touched down on 7 May. Secrecy before the operations began meant that only a handful of people at the base knew what was happening. As Kalra exited his jet after his mission, an airman noticed the empty weapons pylon.

'He pointed to where the missiles should have been and asked, "Sir, *yeh kahaan gaye?* [Sir, where have these gone?]" The poor chap had no access [to the military operations]. So I said, "*Yeh gaye jahaan jaane chahiye thé* [These have gone where they needed to go]."'

The IAF technician got the message instantly, his face radiant with pride. This was what they had spent their entire career training for. Missiles had been fired in anger. But there was something the technician regretted – something he wished he'd been allowed to do.

'*Arrey* Sir, missile *per likhne toh dete!* [Sir, you should have let us write a message on the missiles!]' the man exclaimed.

Kalra's response captured the spirit of those three days perfectly: 'I said, "You are now allowed to write on all the missiles – whatever you feel – go berserk, go unhindered, and be innovative in writing whatever you want to write for the adversary."'

Go berserk. Go unhindered. Write whatever you want for the adversary.

That was the attitude throughout the IAF – from the pilots volunteering for the most dangerous missions to the ground crews preparing aircraft under wartime conditions to the technicians who wanted to send personal messages to Pakistan etched on the warheads themselves.

When war broke out, the fighter pilot had spoken to his eight-year-old daughter from the base. She asked him a question that cut straight to his heart:

'*Papa, aap kab jaoge ladai ladne?* [Papa, when will you go to fight the war?]'

Kalra, like so many officers and men of the IAF, was bound by a code of secrecy. He couldn't tell her what he already knew – that within hours he'd be in the cockpit, weapons hot, pushing deep into hostile airspace.

Three days later, on 10 May, after it had all ended and the ceasefire had been announced, he was finally able to tell her the truth.

He – and all the men and women in the IAF – had gone to fight.

Conclusion

On 10 May, hours after the ceasefire took hold, a senior government official gathered a handful of leading editors for a closed-door briefing. The official, who chose not to be identified, had a message to hammer home, repeatedly: India's goal was to strike terror targets. Terror targets alone.

'We have gone for the head of the snake, not for soldiers,' the official stated.

That may have been the calculus India prepared with. But within 30 minutes of India's attacks on nine terror targets in Pakistan and Pakistan-occupied Kashmir on 7 May, Islamabad choose to see things very differently — as an assault on its territory that demanded direct military retaliation against Indian forces, in the air and on the ground.

What followed was unprecedented escalation between two nuclear-armed neighbors, near-peers as rival air forces, locked in the most hostile, targeted exchanges since the 1971 India–Pakistan war.

Shortly after the IAF and Indian Army commenced their attacks at 1.05 a.m. on 7 May on nine sites – some just across the LoC, others more than a km inside Pakistan proper – India's Director General of Military Operations picked up a dedicated hotline to his Pakistani counterpart.

This hotline, located in the Military Operations Directorate in South Block, is the final direct link between the militaries of both sides – a critical system manned 24/7, 365 days a year. In the early hours of 7 May 2025, Lieutenant General Rajiv Ghai called Major General Kashif Abdullah with a clear message: 'We have done this – attacked terror targets – and we are ready to talk. We are not interested in escalation.'

Ghai was rebuffed. Pakistan wasn't willing to talk. The message was clear: Pakistan's Armed Forces would now respond as they deemed fit. In fact, that response was already underway – the air forces of both sides were already locked in battle by the time the DGMOs spoke.

New Delhi's position was unambiguous: if Islamabad struck militarily, India would climb the escalation ladder – believing a threshold of warfare exists beneath the subcontinent's nuclear umbrella. 'India will not bow down to Pakistan's nuclear blackmail,' Foreign Minister Dr S. Jaishankar told Parliament on 28 July.[25]

India's Chief of Defence Staff, General Anil Chauhan, went further. In his address in June on India's Evolving National Security Landscape, the CDS said, 'In the spectrum of conflict, nuclear conflict lies at the extreme end. My understanding is that nuclear weapons are tools of deterrence, not for war-fighting. India has made it clear it will not be deterred by nuclear blackmail. Operation Sindoor is the only example of a conflict between two nuclear-weapon states.'

General Chauhan's beliefs starkly contrast with those of Pakistan Army Chief and self-appointed Field Marshal, Syed Asim Munir. Speaking in Tampa, Florida, on 10 August 2025, Munir issued an astounding threat: 'We are a nuclear nation. If Pakistan faces an existential threat in a future war with India, we will take half the world down with us.'[26]

The remark – issued from US soil against a third country – underscored catastrophic escalation potential, including nuclear exchange. On 18 October, speaking at the Pakistan Military Academy, Munir added: 'There is no space for war in a nuclearised environment.'[27] His remarks, which New Delhi has consistently believed to be a bluff, align with Pakistan's 'full-spectrum deterrence' doctrine, which allows the use of tactical nuclear weapons in response to conventional threats.

On the night of 9 May, as Indian forces prepared for their most devastating strikes yet, US Vice President J.D. Vance repeatedly tried to reach Prime Minister Narendra Modi. For almost an hour, the calls went unanswered. Modi was in a meeting with India's Armed Forces, making final decisions on targets deep inside Pakistan.

When Prime Minister Modi finally called back, Vance delivered urgent intelligence: Pakistan was planning a major attack, a dramatic escalation. US intelligence had picked up on the preparations.

The Indian Prime Minister's response was unequivocal, and he would later recount it publicly to Parliament: 'If Pakistan intends to carry out such an attack, it will have to pay a very heavy price. That's exactly what I told the US Vice President.'[28]

India's decision to hit major Pakistani military targets on the night of 9–10 May may have been a pre-emptive response to that very phone call. Within hours, Indian strikes devastated Pakistan's premier airbases – Rafiqui, Murid, Sargodha, Jacobabad, Bholari, Rahim Yar Khan and Sukkur. But the clearest signal was Nur Khan Airbase, just 10 km northwest of Islamabad. 'It's like trying to hit Palam.'

The message to Pakistan's leadership left nothing to imagination.

At 3.35 p.m. on 10 May 2025 – less than 24 hours after the devastating Indian strikes on Pakistani airbases – the hotline in South Block rang again.

This time, it was Pakistan's DGMO calling India. Major General Kashif Abdullah's message was simple: Pakistan wanted a ceasefire. Immediately.

During the call, Abdullah was told in no uncertain terms that India would respond to future Pakistani terror attacks – always. This was the new normal. 'The cost for Pakistan will rise inexorably. Actions will have consequences,' Ghai told Abdullah bluntly. The ceasefire would need to be immediate. Both sides agreed to end firing at 5.00 p.m. on 10 May, less than two hours after the conversation.

But the reality was more precarious than official statements suggested.

At the very moment the ceasefire was announced, several IAF fighters were already airborne – armed with orders to strike multiple targets deep inside Pakistan.

'We had plans, but by then other things were happening,' Air Marshal Tiwari recalls. 'So we didn't really go through. If it had escalated, it would have been different.'

Later that afternoon, Foreign Secretary Vikram Misri issued a terse four-sentence statement: 'The Director General of Military Operations of Pakistan called the Director General of Military Operations of India at 1535 hours IST earlier today. It was agreed between them that both sides would stop all firing and military action on land and in the air and sea with effect from 1700 hours Indian Standard Time today. Instructions have been given on both sides to give effect to the understanding. The Directors General of Military Operations will talk again on the 12th of May at 1200 hours.'[29]

Pakistan's Foreign Minister Ishaq Dar echoed: 'Pakistan and India have agreed to a ceasefire with immediate effect. Pakistan has always strived for peace and security in the region, without compromising on its sovereignty and territorial integrity.'[30]

But the ceasefire didn't hold.

Pakistani drone activity over Indian airspace

continued, prompting sharp warnings from New Delhi. The Indian Army resumed shelling Pakistani targets along the LoC and the international border in Jammu. At 11.00 p.m. – six hours after the ceasefire was meant to begin – Misri issued another statement: 'Over the past three hours, there have been repeated violations of the understanding arrived at earlier this evening between the Directors General of Military Operations of India and Pakistan. This is a breach of the understanding arrived at earlier today. The armed forces are giving an adequate and appropriate response to these violations and we take very, very serious notice of these violations.'[31]

The statement came two hours after Jammu and Kashmir Chief Minister Omar Abdullah tweeted: 'What the hell just happened to the ceasefire? Explosions heard across Srinagar.'[32]

It took another two days for the situation to stabilise along the Indo-Pak boundary, with several countries calling for restraint.

Even as the guns fell silent, another battle was beginning – over who could claim credit for stopping the war.

At 5.30 p.m. IST on 10 May, President Donald Trump posted on social media: 'After a long night of talks mediated by the United States, I am pleased to announce that India and Pakistan have agreed to a FULL AND IMMEDIATE CEASEFIRE. Congratulations to both Countries on using Common Sense and Great Intelligence. Thank you for your attention to this matter!'[33]

New Delhi flatly rejected the claim.

At the closed-door briefing with editors, the senior official was explicit: 'Shuttle diplomacy was not encouraged by New Delhi.' The official was emphatic about what had actually forced Pakistan's hand: 'The force of Indian Armed Forces showed them that this was not going to be a winning proposition.'

On 12 May, Prime Minister Modi addressed the nation, making it unmistakably clear that Operation Sindoor was on pause. It wasn't over.

'India struck at the heart of Pakistan. India's drones and missiles attacked with precision. They damaged those airbases of the Pakistani Air Forces [*sic*], of which Pakistan was very proud. India caused heavy damage to Pakistan in the first three days itself, which it had never imagined. That's why after India's aggressive action, Pakistan started looking for ways to escape. Pakistan was pleading to the world to ease tensions. And after suffering heavy losses, Pakistan's Army contacted our

DGMO on the afternoon of tenth May. By then we had destroyed the infrastructure of terrorism on a large scale. The terrorists were eliminated. We had destroyed the terror camps established in the heart of Pakistan. Therefore, when Pakistan appealed and said that it will not indulge in any sort of terror activities or military audacity further, India considered it. And I am repeating again, we have just suspended our retaliatory action against Pakistan's terror and military camps. In the coming days we will measure every step of Pakistan on the criterion that what sort of attitude Pakistan will adopt ahead.'[34]

Nearly two months later, on 29 July, Modi addressed Parliament to directly counter Trump's mediation claims:

'No leader in the world asked India to stop its operation. On the night of the 9 May 2025 – during that time – the Vice President of the United States tried to get in touch with me. He kept trying for almost an hour, but I was in a meeting with our armed forces and couldn't take his call. Later, I called him back. He informed me that Pakistan was planning a major attack. That's what he told me directly. My response was clear: if Pakistan intends to carry out such an attack, it will have to pay a very heavy price.

That's exactly what I told the US Vice President.'[35]

The implication was clear: America had provided warnings, not mediation. India had acted pre-emptively, not reactively. And Pakistan had sued for peace not because of diplomacy, but because of devastating military strikes.

At the NDTV Defence Conclave in New Delhi on 30 August, Air Marshal Tiwari quantified the impact: 'Less than 50 weapons had been fired by the Indian Air Force to achieve conflict termination.'

The conflict proved several game-changing realities about modern warfare in South Asia.

Standoff weaponry has fundamentally altered combat. With missiles capable of hitting targets hundreds of kilometres away, neither side may ever need to cross the LoC again. If jets are shot down, pilots eject over friendly territory – no prisoners of war. But the lethality of new weapons offers little consolation.

For Pakistan, the Chinese PL-15 air-to-air missile and J-10 fighter – equipped with advanced AESA radar – proved to be of significance. For India, the Russian S-400 surface-to-air missile system achieved what observers thought impossible: a 314-km kill – a world record that exceeded even Russian performance in Ukraine. Combined with the Israeli MR-SAM (Barak 8), India's air defence grid became both first and last lines of defence against high-speed Pakistani cruise missiles like the CM-400.

India also operationalised the indigenous BrahMos. While the IAF has never confirmed the weapons deployed on individual targets, it is likely that the Israeli Rampage, Crystal Maze, and European SCALP were deployed in combat. Years of simulated training were validated in actual strikes. Each missile costs several million dollars, making live-fire training in peacetime virtually impossible. Instead, launches are almost always simulated – which is never the same as a live mission with actual weapons release.

'These specialist weapons need immense planning,' says Group Captain Kunal Kalra, the Vir Chakra-winning Flight Commander who led attacks on 7 May. 'They need a lot of flying accuracy as well. You get only a couple of seconds to achieve launch parameters. In those few seconds, you have to be absolutely perfect for the weapon to launch from the aircraft. Unlike unguided dumb bombs, which are released the instant the trigger is pressed, smart weapons require a specific set of parameters to be achieved before release. Such missiles possess substantial computing capability and interact continuously with the aircraft. There is a lot of planning. These weapons also have their own brain. The weapon interacts with the aircraft and both need to match. If both are in sync, there's no stopping it.'

Perhaps the biggest takeaway: drones in combat, deployed at unprecedented scale.

India spearheaded drone deployment in escalating waves from 7 to 10 May. Several Indian Army strikes on Pakistani terror camps narrowly across the LoC involved attack drones in addition to precision shelling using guided projectiles from 155 mm artillery guns. Subsequently, in response to Pakistan's massive drone deployment, India leaned heavily on Israeli-origin Harop loitering munitions for suppression of enemy air defences. The initial wave of Harops targeted radar sites near Lahore, striking parts of Pakistan's air defence network and injuring four soldiers.

Beyond combat, drones like the Indian Army and Air Force's Israeli-manufactured Searcher and Heron provided real-time intelligence, surveillance and reconnaissance, mapping camouflaged targets through high-resolution imagery.

Pakistan, which dubbed its operations Operation Bunyan-um-Marsoos, unleashed upwards of 1,000 drones of all types – from small civilian drones to Turkish-made Asisguard Songar quadcopters armed for kamikaze roles. According to the IAF, on 8 May, Pakistan deployed 300 drones. On the night of 8 May into 9 May, 'increased pan-front drone activity' saw Pakistani forces use 600 drones – a mix of commercial and military drones. These were the ones detected by India's integrated air defence grid – the actual number was likely much higher.

While multiple drones were shot down or jammed, the effort at saturating India's defenses through sheer volume was a key Pakistani tactic during Operation Sindoor.

India released overwhelming visual proof of its strikes – drone footage, satellite imagery from ISRO and commercial provider Maxar (now Vantor). This proved a significant force-multiplier: visual evidence of India's claims, including ISRO-sourced satellite images of hit areas and live video feeds from drones as they approached targets.

Video or satellite imagery of actual Indian cross-border activity has historically been rare. It first emerged in 1999 with the IAF's first successful laser-guided bomb hit on Tiger Hill, a story which I broke at the time. In 2016, grainy footage showed Indian Army Para (Special Forces) – or Para SF – in surgical strikes across the LoC. In 2019, there was no video of the IAF's Balakot strike and only a single relatively low-resolution satellite image.

Operation Sindoor was different.

Independent analysis by experts including Damien Symon, among the world's foremost satellite imagery analysts, confirmed destroyed hangars, cratered runways and obliterated command centres, and underground facilities penetrated by bunker-busters. Penetrator weapons had pierced building roofs at PAF bases. Surface-to-air missile installations had been struck, radars taken out.

Three months after the fighting, on 9 August, Air Chief Marshal A.P. Singh detailed the damage at the 16th Air Chief Marshal L.M. Katre Memorial Lecture in Bengaluru, and repeated these claims with added detail at his annual press conference on 3 October:

'We have at least five Pakistani fighters as confirmed kills and one large aircraft, which could be either an ELINT or AEW&C aircraft, which was taken out at a distance of about 300 km. This is the record for the largest (longest) range at which a surface-to-air kill has been achieved.'[36]

He spelled out the full extent: 'From various intelligence reports, we have gathered that radars were damaged at four locations, command-and-control centres destroyed at two, and runways at two airfields were hit. Three hangars were also damaged across different stations. Within these hangars and on the tarmac, we have clear evidence of one C-130 class aircraft destroyed, along with four to five F-16 fighter jets.'

In total, the IAF claimed to have destroyed 9–10 Pakistani fighters – including US-origin F-16s and Chinese JF-17s – plus at least two special aircraft, counting both air and ground kills.

When I asked Air Marshal Bharti why these were not reported during the war, he replied, 'There is a very good reason. We wanted to be absolutely sure. We did not have any debris to buttress our claim, so we needed to be absolutely sure. We went through our electronic evidence on the basis of which we have come out with what we have.'

Pakistan claimed multiple Indian Rafale kills and shared images of the alleged downed aircraft via social media. But at publication of this book, not a single authenticated satellite image showed damage to Indian airbases – no cratered runways, no destroyed infrastructure.

The IAF refused engagement in a narrative battle with Pakistan. 'We are in a combat scenario, losses are part of combat,' said Air Marshal Bharti. 'The question you must ask us is, have we achieved our objective of decimating the terrorist camps? And the answer is a thumping yes. And the results are for the whole world to see. All our pilots are back home' – indicated no IAF pilot was killed in air combat.

Foreign Secretary Vikram Misri characterised Pakistan's claims as 'a tissue of lies', accusing Islamabad of concocting false narratives about damage to Indian infrastructure. 'Claims have been made about large sections of Indian critical infrastructure, power systems, cyber systems being attacked and destroyed. These are completely false.'

India publicly stated that 26 locations were targeted by Pakistani drones, missiles, loitering munitions and airstrikes in the early hours of 10 May, including Udhampur, Pathankot, Bathinda, Bhuj and Adampur airbases. Drones and armed UAVs had been spotted in Baramulla, Srinagar, Avantipora, Jammu, Pathankot, Bhuj and Jaisalmer. According to Army spokesperson Colonel Sofiya Qureshi: 'They attacked health facilities and schools in Srinagar, Avantipora and Udhampur. These actions represent a dangerous escalation that violates every accepted convention.'

IAF officers extensively interviewed for this account, including the Commander of the Adampur-based S-400 surface-to-air missile unit, categorically denied their systems were hit or rendered inoperative during any Pakistani air strike between 7 and 10 May.

The real metric: effect based operations, absence of collateral damage and precision strikes

Media narratives fixated on scorecards – downed jets, drone swarms. But the actual metrics effect based operations, absence of collateral damage and precision strikes.

Over three intense nights, both sides flew over 1,000 combat sorties – a tempo rarely seen since the 1991 Gulf War. The IAF leveraged its IACCS, fusing data from dozens of radars, AWACS aircraft and ground-based sensors to create a single operational picture updated in real time. This enabled dynamic targeting of Pakistani drone swarms, fighters and missile salvos within seconds of detection.

Pakistan's Air Defence Operations Centre, upgraded with Chinese radars and Turkish data links, achieved similar fusion, allowing real-time re-tasking of fighter aircraft armed with the PL-15E beyond-visual-range air-to-air missile.

Neither India nor Pakistan achieved full air superiority in the initial phase of the conflict. Though both sides engaged in efforts at degrading each other's war-fighting capability, the IAF was able to out-last the PAF in combat operations after successfully taking out key Pakistani terror training facilities – the primary objective of Operation Sindoor.

After a JF-17 fighter was engaged and shot down by an S-400 missile on 7 May, the PAF withdrew westwards, attempting to avoid the kill zone of the long-range Indian surface to air missile system.

In the days that followed the strikes on terror centres on Pakistani soil, the IAF responded to missile attacks by striking and significantly damaging primary Pakistani airbases, surface to air missile units and radar installations.

Through the 88 hours of active conflict, the IAF was also able to withstand sustained drone operations by the PAF, an unprecedented challenge in warfare in the subcontinent.

The IAF is also on record to state that multiple Pakistani fighter jets and a front-line Airborne Electronic Warning and Control Aircraft (or possible a large Electronic Intelligence Platform) were shot down by its surface to air missile units.

By the evening of 9 May, it appeared that the IAF was in a position to strike frontline Pakistan Air Force bases at will.

With key runways cratered, command systems destroyed, radars eliminated and precious fighters obliterated in their hangars, Pakistan's military establishment chose to bring an end to the military hostilities at a stage when the Indian Air Force appeared to be clearly on the ascendency.

'On the morning of May 10, certain instructions were given to all three branches of the armed forces regarding what would happen if this war escalated,' said the Army Chief General Upendra Dwivedi at his annual press conference on 13 January 2026. 'Those who needed to understand it, understood it. They [Pakistan] had complete information from satellites about which ship, which strike or pivot, which core unit, or which aircraft was moving where – when they connected the dots, they said that the time has come to stop this war here.'

This outcome of the 88-hour war was perhaps inevitable. As a significantly larger, better equipped and more capable military power, the IAF was able to prove that it has a greater capacity to attack, sustain operations and absorb losses in a conventional conflict. Media narratives remained fixated on 'downed jets' and 'drone swarms' as trophies, but the real metric was operational sustainability. In that, the PAF fell short.

For New Delhi, the goal of Operation Sindoor was to send a clear message that Pakistani-sponsored terrorism would be countered. The strikes on terror targets – the most expansive in India's military history – were clearly successful but hardly indicate terrorism emanating from Pakistan-based groups has ended.

New Delhi knows this. 'This is a new normal,' said the senior official briefing editors. 'It is not business as usual. There is no place in Pakistan safe for those who engage in terrorism.'

Modi's message was explicit: India has suspended retaliatory action. Not ended it. The subcontinent will be shaped by what Pakistan does next.

Despite claims and counterclaims, what remains clear is that the use of air power in the subcontinent has dramatically changed. Standoff weaponry probably means war planners on either side may never feel the need to order pilots to physically cross the LoC or international border to hit targets. The success of sophisticated weapons systems – from the S-400 to the BrahMos to drones at unprecedented scale – validated years of training and billions in defence spending.

Unlike other recent air battles, this was not one-sided. Both forces came at each other with intensity and intent, not unlike previous wars in 1965, 1971 or 1999. Modern air warfare is not a T-20 match with instant gratification. Losses of soldiers and platforms are neither unusual nor unexpected.

While Operation Sindoor demonstrated that limited conventional war between nuclear-armed states is possible, it also proved something else: the threshold beneath the nuclear umbrella is real, but precarious. Pakistan's nuclear threats didn't deter India. India's conventional superiority forced Pakistan to seek a ceasefire. But the underlying tensions – terrorism, territorial disputes, nuclear brinkmanship – remain unresolved.

Which is why the subcontinent will continue to remain tense. Operation Sindoor isn't over. It's on pause.

In a key assessment of Operation Sindoor, India's Deputy Chief of Army Staff (Capability Development and Sustenance), Lieutenant General Rahul R Singh, revealed that the conflict with Pakistan was far from a straightforward bilateral affair.

India effectively faced three adversaries on a single front: Pakistan as the primary opponent, backed by substantial support from China and, to a notable extent, Turkey. In a talk on emerging military technologies in New Delhi on 4 July, Lieutenant General Singh highlighted a troubling aspect of the escalation – China's active role extended well beyond arms supplies. He stated that during critical Director General of Military Operations (DGMO)-level talks aimed at de-escalation on 10 May, it appeared that Pakistan received live, real-time updates on Indian military deployments and movements directly from China. Pakistani representatives reportedly referenced specific Indian 'vectors' (key assets or positions) that were primed and ready, urging India to pull them back. This appeared to indicate clear evidence of ongoing intelligence sharing from Beijing.

'We had one border and two adversaries, actually three,' Lieutenant General Singh explained. 'Pakistan was in the front. China was providing all possible support ... When DGMO-level talks were on, Pakistan had the live updates of our important vectors, from China.'

He further pointed out that 81 per cent of Pakistan's military hardware is of Chinese origin, turning the country into what he described as a 'live lab' for Beijing.

According to data from the Stockholm International Peace Research Institute (SIPRI), China has supplied Pakistan with arms worth $8.2 billion since 2015. Between 2020 and 2024, nearly two-thirds (63 per cent) of China's total arms exports went to Pakistan, making it Beijing's largest weapons client by far.

Lieutenant General Singh also noted Turkey's involvement, particularly in supplying drones and other support that added complexity to the battlefield. The revelations underscore a growing strategic axis among China, Pakistan and Turkey, posing a multi-dimensional challenge for India's security planning.

Sadly, six months later, on 10 November, the Red Fort – a bastion of national pride – shook under a suicide car bomb's fury. Fifteen people were killed and

20 injured in the blast in the heart of Old Delhi – one of the most congested parts of India's NCR. This was the first major terror strike on Delhi since the 2011 Delhi High Court bombing, in which fifteen were killed.

In the Red Fort attack, a white Hyundai i20, packed with ammonium nitrate erupted at a traffic signal opposite Chandni Chowk, shredding tourists and commuters alike. Investigations by the National Investigation Agency (NIA) have revealed a Kashmir-linked plot, with the bomber, Dr Umar Nabi, and accomplices plotting Mumbai 26/11-style assaults on landmarks like India Gate.

Op Sindoor's thunder may have been a response to the Pahalgam terror attack but the roots of Pakistani-terrorism still exist. The roots of terror, nurtured in Bahawalpur's rebuilt shadows, slithered through intelligence chinks. Despite heightened alerts and arrests, the attack exposed vulnerabilities: porous supply chains for explosives, radicalised insiders and the resilience of jihadist networks.

The blood on Red Fort's shadow underscored a grim truth: one operation cannot cauterise an ideology. Vigilance must evolve, or terror's echo will reverberate again.

Appendix

Key Targets Struck by the Indian Air Force

Terror targets struck in Bahawalpur and Muridke: 7 May, 1.05 a.m.

- **Jaish-e-Mohammed (JeM) headquarters, Bahawalpur, Punjab province:** The Bahawalpur site (Markaz Subhan Allah) has been historically linked to JeM, the group responsible for the 2001 Indian Parliament House attack and the 2019 Pulwama bombing.
- **Lashkar-e-Taiba (LeT) in Muridke, Punjab province:** The Muridke complex (Markaz Taiba, under the façade of Jamaat-ud-Dawa [JuD]) is the known command-and-control centre for LeT, which orchestrated the 2008 Mumbai attacks.

Radar and surface-to-air missile installations: 7–10 May

- **Chunian:** A radar head was hit – imagery indicates burn marks on its structure.
- **Arifwala**: Radar installation – imagery indicates a blackened crater.
- **Pasrur**: An air-defence radar – imagery indicates missile impact craters.

Multiple PAF bases and infrastructure: 10 May, 2.00–5.00 a.m.

- Chaklala, Rahawali, Rafiqui, Rahim Yar Khan, Sukkur, Murid, Nayachor attacked with missiles.

Multiple PAF bases and infrastructure: 10 May, 10.00 a.m.–12.00 p.m.

- Sargodha, Bholari and Jacobabad attacked with missiles.

Major IAF strikes: Verified with satellite imagery

Muridke in Punjab province

Around 30 km north of Lahore and roughly 18–25 km inside Pakistani territory, the sprawling Markaz Taiba complex functioned for years as Lashkar-e-Taiba's principal headquarters. Established in 2000 and spread across more than 200 acres, the site housed facilities for weapons training, physical conditioning, intelligence work and ideological indoctrination. Several perpetrators of the 2008 Mumbai attacks, including Ajmal Kasab, are known to have trained here. Parts of the complex, including a mosque and guesthouse, were reportedly funded by Osama bin Laden.

The strikes were executed with clinical precision. Multiple missiles struck the compound over a span of several minutes, destroying critical structures. Post-strike satellite imagery released by Maxar Technologies showed extensive damage: collapsed roofs punctured by large penetration holes, administrative buildings reduced to debris and adjacent structures such as the Jamia Ummul Qura mosque suffering partial dome collapse and blast craters.

Ground reports spoke of scattered shrapnel, blown-in doors and obliterated residential sections, with solar panels and bricks strewn across the site. Four principal impact points hit key operational nodes, while surrounding areas were largely spared, indicating deliberate efforts to limit collateral damage. The destruction effectively crippled LeT's core training and radicalisation infrastructure, long described as a 'terror nursery' despite international sanctions.

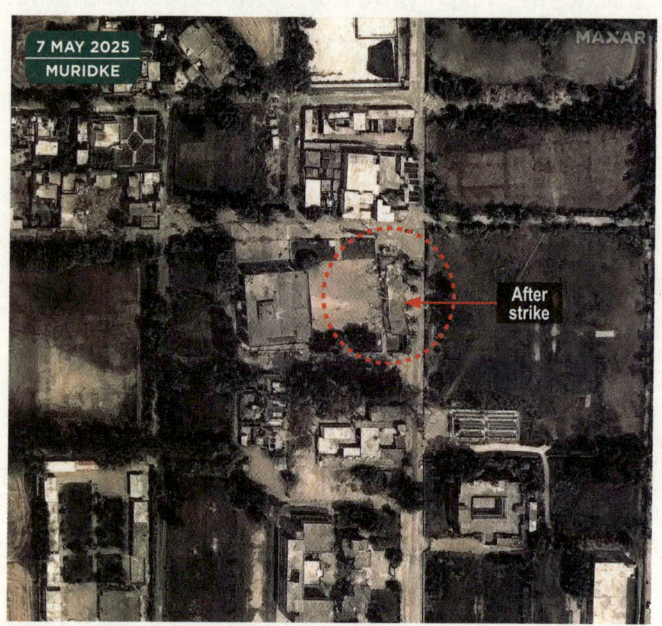

Satellite image ©2025 Maxar Technologies

Bahawalpur

Approximately 100 km inside Pakistan and representing the deepest penetration of the operation – the Markaz Subhan Allah complex served as Jaish-e-Mohammed's operational headquarters. Spread across 15–18 acres along the Karachi–Torkham Highway, the facility included a large mosque, leadership residences, and infrastructure for recruitment, fundraising, arms training, and religious indoctrination.

Founded by Masood Azhar, a Bahawalpur native, the complex remained active despite UN sanctions, routinely hosting anti-India rhetoric and operational planning. Indian forces employed advanced precision-guided munitions to strike the site directly. Satellite imagery comparing pre- and post-strike conditions revealed dramatic changes: three mosque domes were pierced or collapsed, while two remained intact, underscoring the accuracy of the strikes.

Surrounding buildings covering more than 2,100 square metres were reduced to rubble, with video footage capturing multiple explosions and expanding debris fields. Key indoctrination and command structures were flattened, and residences linked to JeM leadership sustained heavy damage, disrupting fundraising networks and cadre mobilisation.

The operation, completed in roughly 25 minutes using air- and ground-launched assets from Indian territory, deliberately avoided Pakistani military installations. It neutralised significant terrorist infrastructure, reportedly eliminating over 100 militants across the targeted sites. Physical evidence – craters, collapsed structures and widespread debris – highlighted the effectiveness of the strikes in degrading entrenched terror hubs deep within Pakistani Punjab, marking a rare escalation since 1971.

Although rebuilding efforts surfaced later under various pretexts, the immediate impact of the strikes severely impaired the operational capabilities of both LeT and JeM.

Photo by Shahid Saeed Mirza/AFP via Getty Images

Bholari: The AWACS kill

Of all the hits on 10 May, two have been most widely highlighted: the strikes on Bholari and Jacobabad. The strike on a green roof in Bholari shows a massive impact likely to have destroyed everything inside the hangar. While the IAF does not identify the weapon which struck any particular target, it is possible that Bholari was struck by a SCALP missile fired by a Rafale fighter.

At the time of attacking Bholari, the IAF did have intelligence which suggested the PAF were operating AEW&C at this base, but they weren't entirely sure that this was in the hangar when it was destroyed. The destruction of this aircraft, likely a SAAB Erieye, was confirmed subsequently through what the IAF Vice Chief, Air Marshal Narmdeshwar Tiwari, identifies as 'inputs'.

'We knew that there is an AWACS hangar out there. And that's what we targeted.'

Significantly, the IAF was absolutely clear – they did not want to attack any area where collateral damage could have taken place. 'We have chosen targets very specifically in terms of taking out his capability. We are not interested in targeting areas where people are there or, it could lead to some collateral [damage].

Source: Satellite image © 2025 Vantor

They cannot accuse us and they have not accused us of, you know, [of having caused] collateral damage.'

The IAF minimised the spread of damage to a wider area despite some of these targets being 300–600 km inside Pakistan – the accuracy of an entirely new generation of air-to-surface weapons was validated in an operational role while in IAF service.

The Chief Minister of Sindh, Murad Ali Shah, in a statement confirmed that six PAF personnel – including an officer – had been killed in the attack on Bholari.

Nur Khan Airbase: The command-and-control strike

Satellite imagery available a few days after the strikes indicated that Pakistan's critical Nur Khan Airbase had suffered far greater destruction from Operation Sindoor than initially reported.

Nur Khan had served as a key centre for Pakistan's drone operations and VIP aircraft, making it a prime strategic asset for the PAF. 'A detailed examination of Nur Khan Airbase showed the entire facility adjacent to the impact zone had been completely razed, indicating the strike's reach had exceeded the two targeted special-purpose vehicles – implying a much wider damage radius,' said Damien Symon, a prominent Geo-intelligence Researcher and Open-Source Intelligence (OSINT) Analyst at the Intel Lab, widely recognised for his expertise in deciphering satellite imagery in conflict zones.

'That was a Command and Control centre,' says Air Marshal Tiwari, referring to the strike on Nur Khan. Other than two special-purpose vehicles that were destroyed, 'We feel that there is probably something underground there also.'

The operation against Nur Khan carried both tactical and symbolic weight, given the base's proximity to Pakistan Army headquarters and its role as the nerve-centre for PAF air mobility through platforms such as C-130 transports and IL-78 aerial refuellers. The base had also stationed Turkish Bayraktar TB2 drones and Pakistan's homegrown Shahpar-I UAVs, integral to reconnaissance and strike capabilities. Nur Khan had underpinned Pakistan's drone-centric warfare doctrine and had accommodated elite pilot training alongside the presidential fleet.

The strike's magnitude had laid bare critical gaps in Pakistan's air defence network. Pakistan Prime Minister Shehbaz Sharif went on to reveal that he had been awakened in the early hours of the morning – with a call at 2.30 a.m. on a secure line – by Army Chief General Syed Asim Munir, who had informed him that India had just launched ballistic missiles and hit multiple airbases, including Nur Khan. There has been no Indian report of the use of ballistic missiles by Indian Armed Forces during Operation Sindoor.

According to Sharif, Pakistan had retaliated by striking Indian locations, including Pathankot and Udhampur.

Pakistan Military Spokesperson Lt Gen. Ahmed Sharif Chaudhry confirmed in a 4 a.m. press conference on 10 May that India had targeted Nur

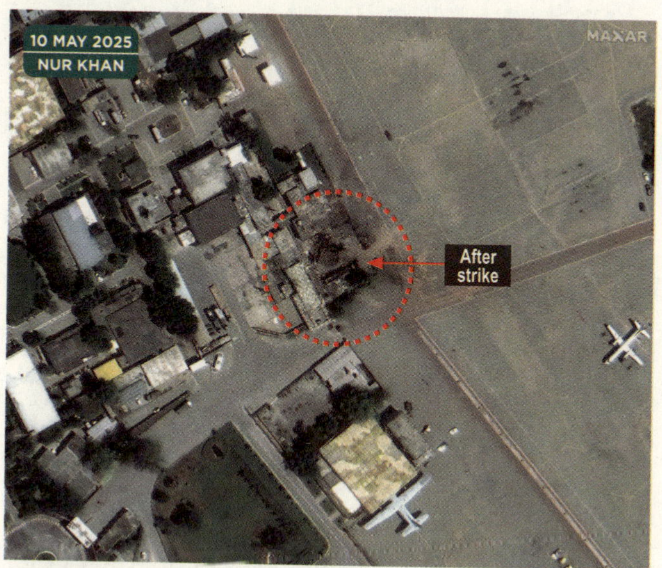

Source. Satellite image © 2025 Vantor

Khan (Rawalpindi), Murid (Chakwal) and Rafiqui (Jhang) airbases. His statement confirmed that Nur Khan had been one of the closest Indian strike points to Islamabad.

Murid: Striking the underground facility

Satellite images showed extensive damage to Pakistan's Murid Airbase, revealing a large crater close to underground facility of the PAF and damage to the rooftop of a structure adjacent to unmanned aerial vehicle hangars.

'The strike was visible at the most guarded complex within Murid Airbase. The approximately 3-m-wide munition-impact crater was just 30 m north of one of the two entrances to a likely underground facility,' says Damien Symon. 'This complex was heavily protected, with double fencing, its own watchtowers and access control, indicating its high-value nature as a target. The earth-protected entrances suggested this site might have served as storage for special equipment or as a hardened operational shelter for personnel, capable of withstanding heavy bombardment,' he adds.

Another image accessed by this author shows damage to a building on the base located next to a drone hub of the PAF. Symon says, 'Structural damage

Satellite image ©2025 Maxar Technologies

was evident at this facility, believed to have served as a command-and-control node near the UAV complex of the airbase. A portion of the roof had collapsed inward, and the outer walls also exhibited visible deterioration, likely from impact-related stress. A strike like this could have also caused damage within the upper floors of the building as well.'

The Murid Airbase is 150 km from the LoC in Jammu and Kashmir. It supports the Sargodha Airbase and the Nur Khan Airbase in Rawalpindi.

Sukkur: Total hangar collapse

The Maxar Technologies (now Vantor) satellite image, dated 10 May 2025, captures a large rectangular hangar structure that has collapsed entirely, exposing internal framework. The walls appear folded inwards, with structural steel beams twisted and displaced. To the east of the damaged hangar, a debris field extends across the concrete apron. Scattered material is likely to include metallic fragments, concrete chunks and twisted rebar.

Debris is concentrated along the eastern edge of the apron and adjacent taxiway. Southwest of the hangar, an area of vegetation shows dark discoloration consistent with burn marks. The affected grass and

Source: Satellite image © 2025 Vantor

scrub appear blackened compared to surrounding green patches.

No aircraft, vehicles or personnel are visible in the satellite image. The base perimeter roads and access points show no activity. The IAF believes that this was a base for unmanned aerial vehicles.

Jacobabad: The F-16 question

Home to the 39 Tactical Wing of the PAF, the Shahbaz Airbase in Jacobabad houses three premier PAF squadrons – two of them F-16 units: the 5 Squadron 'Falcons' and the 11 Squadron 'Arrows'. A third unit, the 88 Squadron 'Rams' operates AW-139 and Mi-17 helicopters.

On 10 May, the Indian Air Force struck a large hangar in Jacobabad which it believes was a key F-16 maintenance facility.

IAF Chief, Air Chief Marshal A.P. Singh stated on 9 August that precision strikes obliterated half the F-16 hangar at Shahbaz Airbase, Jacobabad, adding: 'I'm sure there were some aircraft inside which have got damaged.' Satellite imagery shows a large part of the roof destroyed with a debris field in the area.

Notably, the US administration has declined to address pointed questions sent in by this author regarding the destruction of F-16 aircraft operated by the PAF amid Operation Sindoor.

In its response to NDTV, the US State Department declared, 'We refer you to the Government of Pakistan to discuss its F-16s.'

The United States possesses comprehensive awareness of the condition of all F-16s in Pakistani service via American contractors, referred to as technical support teams (TSTs), stationed permanently in Pakistan to oversee the deployment of these US-manufactured fighters around the clock.

These TSTs function under detailed end-use protocols established between Islamabad and Washington. The protocols outline the permissible combat scenarios for Pakistan's F-16s and form the foundation for ongoing American assistance in maintaining and supporting the fleet.

Consequently, the technical support teams are required by contract to maintain complete, real-time knowledge of the whereabouts and operational status of every F-16 in Pakistan's inventory.

The US State Department's reply to NDTV stands in sharp contrast to the details about Pakistani F-16s that US officials shared with *Foreign Policy* magazine in 2019, soon after India's airstrikes on the Balakot terrorist site.

At that juncture, in response to similar inquiries, *Foreign Policy* magazine quoted, 'Two senior US defence officials with direct knowledge of the situation told *Foreign Policy* that US personnel recently counted Islamabad's F-16s and found none missing.'[37] This statement followed India's assertion that a PAF F-16 had been downed during the engagement.

'We know that there were F-16s inside,' says Air Marshal Narmdeshwar Tiwari, responding in the affirmative when asked specifically whether this information was available before the IAF strikes went in, or whether this was a conclusion arrived at subsequently, as in the case of Bholari where the IAF subsequently reached the conclusion that an AEW&C platform was destroyed.

Asked specifically if the IAF knew there were F-16s inside before the strikes went in, Air Marshal Tiwari said, 'There would be aircraft inside. Our sense

Source: Satellite image © 2025 Vantor

is that [that] at least four to five aircraft. Because [of] the kind of weapons, the calibre and that explosive – it's taken out that entire thing. Inside everything is gone – shattered.'

Rahim Yar Khan: The diverted strike

Maxar (now Vantor) satellite imagery from 10 May 2025 shows the 3,000 m runway (01/19) at Rahim Yar Khan Airbase in southern Punjab, Pakistan.

The image captures a dark-grey blast crater located at the runway centreline, 1,100 m from the southern threshold.

The crater measures 5.8 m in depth and is believed to be 13 m in diameter. Debris, including concrete fragments, asphalt pieces and dark soot, scatters radially over a 40 m radius.

Stress fractures extend outwards from the crater edge, reaching up to 25 m in all directions. The impact severs the white centre-line marking and adjacent edge stripes. Parallel drainage ditches, irrigation canals and surrounding agricultural fields with visible crop patterns are present on both sides.

'We were not originally planning to hit [Rahim Yar Khan] but we got inputs that they are going to be used for offensive action,' says Air Marshal Tiwari.

Source: Satellite image © 2025 Vantor

'Otherwise Rahim Yar Khan is largely a civil airport, which is [a] small civil terminal and they have got four or five parking spots for military aircraft. But it's not one of the main bases. But since we had this input that it is likely to be used, so we did divert one strike to take that out.'

Sargodha: The double crater

Maxar satellite imagery captured on 10 May 2025 shows PAF Base Mushaf (Sargodha) in Punjab, Pakistan, with its primary 3,200 m runway (10/28) and intersecting taxiways.

The image focuses on the southern taxiway–runway junction. There is a fresh, dark-grey blast crater which sits exactly at the intersection, measuring approximately 8–9 m wide and 4–5 m deep. The crater interrupts the white centre-line of the main runway and the dashed taxiway markings.

There appear to be ejected asphalt and concrete fragments which lie scattered. Several ground vehicles – three yellow construction trucks, one white pickup and two red fire-response units – are parked 50–80 m north of the crater, facing the damage.

Source: Satellite image © 2025 Vantor

The surrounding apron remains intact, with hardened shelters and perimeter roads undamaged. There is a second identical crater 1,200 m farther north on the main runway – with roughly the same dimensions and debris fan. The dual craters sever the full length of the operational surface.

Key IAF and PAF Fighters and Missile Systems

IAF Advanced Systems

Sukhoi-30 MKI

The Su-30 MKI is more than just a multirole fighter; it is a strategic deep-strike platform due to its size and massive payload capacity of up to 8,000 kg on its 12 hardpoints. Its key technical differentiator is its thrust vectoring control (TVC), enabled by its two AL-31FP engines, which allows the exhaust nozzles to swivel in the pitch plane. This capacity allows the fighter to execute extreme manoeuvres, which are tactically useful in close-in combat, and enables pilots to break the lock of enemy radars and heat-seeking missiles. This feature, combined with its canards (small fore-wings), gives it unparalleled agility. Its primary radar is the Russian N011M Bars passive electronically scanned array (PESA), a hybrid system that can be electronically steered and mechanically slewed. Although older technology than AESA radars, it provides excellent range and the ability to track 15 targets and engage four of them simultaneously at ranges believed to be in excess of

150 km. The IAF has integrated a mix of Western and Israeli avionics, and an Israeli-made helmet-mounted display, transforming it into a uniquely customised hybrid combat system.

Dassault Rafale

The Rafale isn't just a fighter jet; it's a truly omnirole aircraft. This means it can instantly switch between radically different missions – such as achieving air superiority, performing precision bombing, attacking ships, conducting reconnaissance or even delivering a nuclear deterrent – all without needing to land, change its physical setup or sacrifice performance.

This incredible versatility is powered by its advanced sensor fusion architecture. The jet acts as a super-smart computer, seamlessly blending data from all its onboard systems into a single, crystal-clear, real-time tactical picture for the pilot.

At the heart of its capability is the Thales RBE2-AA AESA radar, one of the most capable fighter radars available. It can detect a fighter-sized target over 200 km away and simultaneously track dozens of air and ground targets. It can create detailed, high-resolution maps of the ground and even track moving vehicles in near real-time. The radar constantly changes its frequency and power in randomised ways, making it almost impossible for an enemy aircraft's radar warning system to even detect that the Rafale is scanning for them. In short, the Rafale can see the threat long before the threat knows it is being watched.

To further enhance its effectiveness in contested airspace, the Rafale has significant defences built in. Its shape, internal weapon layout and use of radar-absorbent materials provide a measure of stealth.

The SPECTRA suite

This is a fully integrated, drag-free electronic warfare (EW) system built right into the airframe. It provides 360-degree coverage, instantly detects threats, locates enemy radars and warns of incoming missiles. Against radar-guided missiles, SPECTRA's advanced jammers create sophisticated fake targets or overwhelming noise. Against heat-seeking missiles, directional laser turrets (DIRCM) can blind the incoming missile's seeker head. When combined with the long-range 'stealthy' AESA radar and its omnirole mission flexibility, the Rafale is one of the most effective and survivable combat jets operating in dangerous environments today.

Mirage 2000 upgrade

The upgraded Mirage 2000 is designated as the Mirage 2000I/TI (I for India, T for trainer). The core of the modernisation package is the Thales RDY-2 pulse-doppler radar. In an air-to-air role, this high-performance radar provides a true multitarget engagement capability, allowing the Mirage to track eight and engage four airborne targets simultaneously. For air-to-ground missions, it offers very high resolution for terrain mapping, using synthetic aperture radar (SAR) mode. The upgrade also introduced a modern glass cockpit with multi-function colour displays, replacing the old analogue gauges and integrated new weapons, most notably the MBDA MICA missile.

Missile and Air Defence System Capabilities

S-400 Triumf

The S-400 Triumf[38] is a complex, networked weapon designed to enforce a massive air denial zone through a multilayered defence. The system's effectiveness is centred on its sophisticated radar array. Long-range surveillance is provided by the 91N6E 'Big Bird' acquisition radar, an L-band phased array system that can detect targets up to 600 km away, tracking up to 300 threats simultaneously. The system also utilises the 96L6E all-altitude detector radar for comprehensive 360-degree coverage against low-flying and low-RCS threats in complex terrain. Once a target is identified, the 92N6E 'Grave Stone' engagement radar takes over as the high-resolution fire-control unit; this X-band radar can lock onto 36 targets and guide missiles to 72 threats concurrently. To execute this multilayered defence, the system deploys four distinct types of interceptors. The 40N6 missile (400 km range) uses a sophisticated active radar seeker (ARS) in its terminal phase, making it a true fire-and-forget weapon and a vital anti-AWACS asset. The 48N6DM (250 km range) targets fighters and cruise missiles, while the highly manoeuvrable 9M96E2 (120 km range) uses a complex gas-dynamic steering system to achieve intense manoeuvres over 20G during its terminal phase. This is designed specifically to destroy precision-guided munitions and high-speed cruise missiles. The shorter-range 9M96E (40 km) handles close-in threats. This combination of radar systems and missile types enables the S-400 to simultaneously target fighter jets, cruise missiles and even short-to medium-range ballistic missile warheads at varying ranges and altitudes.

MBDA Meteor

The Meteor[39] is the next-generation beyond-visual-range air-to-air missile (BVRAAM) integrated into the IAF's Rafale fleet, representing a major kinetic leap in air dominance. Its world-beating performance is achieved through its unique solid-fuel throttleable ducted rocket (ramjet) engine. Unlike conventional rocket motors that provide a rapid but finite burst of speed, the ramjet uses atmospheric oxygen to provide sustained thrust all the way to target intercept, allowing the missile to cruise at speeds of over Mach 4. This sustained velocity maintains the missile's energy and generates the largest no-escape zone (NEZ) of any current BVRAAM system, making it nearly impossible for an agile aircraft to kinetically evade the missile even at extended ranges. It is further enhanced by an advanced active radar seeker and a two-way data link that allows for mid-course guidance (MCG) updates from the launch platform or an AWACS, enabling the pilot to use the 'launch-and-dump' tactic and ensuring a high probability of kill even against targets manoeuvring in a heavy electronic countermeasures environment.

SCALP (Storm Shadow)

The SCALP[40] is characterised by its meticulous mission planning process. Before launch, the missile is programmed with a detailed three-dimensional flight path based on satellite intelligence and sophisticated terrain contour matching (TERCOM) data. It flies at a low, subsonic speed at extremely low altitude to evade radar detection, using its internal inertial navigation system (INS) and GPS. The missile's terminal phase involves a steep climb before diving on the target. This ensures the powerful BROACH (Bomb Royal Ordnance Augmented Charge) warhead strikes vertically or near-vertically, maximising the effect of its tandem charge. The BROACH system uses a first-stage shaped charge to blast a hole through the hardened layer, before a time-delayed, follow-through main penetrator flies through and detonates inside the target structure.

Air-Launched BrahMos

The Air-Launched BrahMos (BrahMos-A) is currently the heaviest weapon carried by the Su-30 MKI, weighing approximately 2.5 tonnes. Its key advantage is its raw supersonic velocity (Mach 2.8 to 3), maintained by a liquid-fuelled ramjet engine that ignites after the initial solid-fuel booster stage. This sustained supersonic flight creates a high level of kinetic energy on impact and makes it virtually impossible for most current ship-based or land-based air defence systems to intercept due to the minimal time available for reaction. After launch, it cruises at supersonic speed, often flying very low (a sea-skimming trajectory for anti-ship roles or a low-altitude profile for land attack) before a possible final manoeuvre toward the target.

The process of BrahMos integration with the Su-30 MKI

Integrating the BrahMos-A onto the Su-30 MKI was a complex and unprecedented engineering feat due to the missile's size and weight.[41] This was not a simple attachment process but a major structural and electronic modification programme, carried out primarily by Hindustan Aeronautics Limited (HAL). The heaviest modification involved structurally reinforcing the airframe of the Su-30 MKI, including strengthening the centre-line pylon that carries the single missile, and reinforcing the landing gear to handle the increased weight during takeoff and landing. The original naval/land variant of the BrahMos was substantially lightened for carriage by the fighter, involving reducing the size of the booster, making the casing thinner and minimising non-essential components. Furthermore, the aircraft's mission computers and fire control system had to be completely rewritten and tested to interface with the missile's complex guidance and pre-launch sequencing software. This ensures the aircraft's systems can accurately load target coordinates and receive status updates from the missile. Finally, an extensive series of carriage, separation and final live firing tests were required, with the critical separation test ensuring the heavy missile drops cleanly from the fuselage before its rocket motor ignites, addressing aerodynamic instability concerns. This lengthy process was necessary to convert the Su-30 MKI into a strategic platform capable of firing the BrahMos at standoff distances.

Rampage

The Rampage[42] is an Israeli-designed long-range, precision air-to-surface missile often referred to as a cost-effective alternative to larger cruise missiles. It is specifically intended for suppression of enemy air defences (SEAD) and destruction of high-value static targets like bunkers, communication centres and radar sites. Flying at a supersonic terminal speed (up to Mach 1.6) and employing a robust Global Positioning System/inertial navigation system (GPS/INS) guidance package, its high velocity upon impact significantly enhances the lethality of its warhead, potentially a multi-explosively formed penetrator (MEFP) warhead, allowing it to penetrate and destroy reinforced concrete structures from a safe launching distance of 150–250 km, keeping the launch aircraft out of range of many ground-based air defences.

Crystal Maze (Popeye Turbo)

The Crystal Maze missile system[43] is the Indian designation for an Israeli-developed standoff air-to-surface cruise missile, formally known as the Popeye Turbo. This precision-guided weapon, developed by Rafael Advanced Defense Systems, is powered by a liquid-fuel turbojet engine, giving it an extended range of up to 320 km. It is intended to be launched from a safe distance (a 'standoff' range) by aircraft like the Mirage 2000, allowing the launch platform to avoid entering hostile air defence zones. It is equipped with an inertial navigation system (INS) and often features a crucial man-in-the-loop terminal guidance option using a television or imaging infrared (IIR) seeker. The image is relayed back to the launch aircraft via a data link, allowing the weapon system operator to correct the target point or abort the mission in the final stages of flight, ensuring high precision against high-value stationary targets with its relatively heavy warhead.

IAF Short- and Medium-Range Weapons

- **MR-SAM:** The newest addition to India's arsenal, this Israeli-designed system can reach out to approximately 70 km. Its robust capability against high-speed manoeuvring targets makes it a formidable threat to anything trying to penetrate Indian airspace.

- **Akash:** An indigenous short- to medium-range system with a 25–30 km reach, the Akash was designed to neutralise aircraft, helicopters and drones with high manoeuvrability. Indian-designed, Indian-built – it is a point of pride for the defence establishment.

- **Spyder:** Another Israeli-derived system, the Spyder uses Python-5 and Derby missiles to engage targets 15–50 km away. All-weather. Rapid response. Purpose-built for low-flying threats like drones and cruise missiles – exactly what Pakistan was throwing at India.

- **Pechora:** A legacy Russian system, but don't let the age fool you. The IAF had substantially upgraded the Pechora with digitisation and enhanced radar to track low RCS targets – the kind of small, sneaky drones now flooding across the border. With a range of 25–35 km, it is expected to remain effective until at least 2030. During Operation Sindoor, it proved its worth.

- **SAMAR:** Perhaps the most ingenious system of all. Indian engineers had taken Russian-built R-73 and R-27 air-to-air missiles from IAF fighters – missiles nearing the end of their shelf-life – and repurposed them as surface-to-air weapons. A quick-reaction system with a reach of approximately 25 km (depending on the missile fired), SAMAR became a drone-killer during Operation Sindoor, successfully engaging low-flying targets that slipped across the LoC and the international border.

PAF Advanced Systems

CAC/PAC JF-17 Thunder Block III

The latest JF-17 Block III represents a major jump to a true 4.5-generation capability.[44] Its most critical feature is the integration of the KLJ-7A AESA radar, which provides a major improvement in detection range, simultaneous multimode operation and resistance to electronic countermeasures (ECM) compared to the older mechanically scanned radars, allowing it to track up to 15 targets and engage four. This is coupled with a helmet-mounted display (HMD) system and an advanced digital fly-by-wire (DFBW) flight control system. The HMD enables the pilot to use high off-boresight missiles like the PL-10 in dogfights, where the pilot can simply look at the target to cue and fire, vastly improving close-in combat capability. It is designed to carry and launch long-range weapons, including the PL-15, making it a critical BVR platform.

Chengdu J-10CE

The J-10CE is the PAF's latest Chinese-made multirole fighter, often compared to the F-16 and Rafale in its class.[45] Its aerodynamic design, featuring a large delta wing and canards in a close-coupled configuration, provides high agility and control at high angles of attack. It is equipped with an advanced Chinese AESA radar (reportedly the KLJ-10) and is known for its extensive use of composites in its airframe, contributing to a lower radar cross-section. Crucially, the J-10CE is fully integrated into the Chinese-developed weapons ecosystem, allowing it to carry the full suite of modern, long-range Chinese munitions, including the PL-15, giving the PAF a highly modern, network-enabled fighting capability.

Lockheed Martin F-16 Fighting Falcon Block 50/52
The F-16 remains a highly capable platform, particularly the Block 50/52 variants. Its core strengths include excellent acceleration, a high turn rate and a mature, combat-tested avionics architecture. Its fly-by-wire (FBW) system and relaxed static stability make it extremely manoeuvrable. The Block 50/52 variants are powered by the General Electric F110 engine and feature the high-resolution APG-68(V)9 radar. For the PAF, the F-16's value lies in its seamless integration with highly effective US-origin weapons like the AIM-120 AMRAAM and Paveway series of guided bombs, which are consistently updated through Foreign Military Sales (FMS) programmes. These variants can also carry the SNIPER Advanced Targeting Pod for high-resolution, long-range

targeting, ensuring it remains at the forefront of US-compatible technology.

Missile and Air Defence System Capabilities

CM-400AKG

The CM-400AKG[46] is a long-range, air-launched missile designed with a sophisticated quasi-ballistic flight profile that is uncharacteristic of standard cruise missiles. It is launched at a high altitude and accelerates to its cruise speed (Mach 2 or more) before potentially achieving ultra-high speeds of Mach 4.5 to Mach 5 in its steep terminal dive. This high-altitude trajectory extends its range while the extreme terminal velocity drastically reduces the time available for enemy air and missile defenses to react, making it exceptionally difficult to intercept. It can use multiple guidance modes, including its passive radar seeker (PRS) for anti-radiation, that is, suppression of enemy air defences (SEAD) and destruction of enemy radar sites, or an IR/TV Seeker for terminal guidance against fixed targets and naval assets, making it a versatile standoff attack weapon primarily carried by the JF-17.

HQ-9

The HQ-9[47] is the core of Pakistan's long-range strategic ground-based air defence (GBAD). A single battery typically consists of a fire control radar (like the HT-233 multifunction radar) and several transporter erector launchers (TELs). The system's strength lies in its ability to operate in a networked battalion-level configuration, which allows multiple batteries and various search radars to share data, creating a wide and resilient air defence coverage. Its advanced command and control (C2) structure enables data-linking of multiple engagement and search radars, ensuring that the destruction of one battery does not collapse the entire defence. It is designed to engage threats up to 100 km or more, operating at the medium- to high-altitude band and providing a critical countermeasure against cruise missiles and high-flying aircraft.

PL-15

The PL-15[48] is considered a major technological leap for the PAF. Its long range, which is maximised by its dual-pulse rocket motor (providing a second burst of thrust in the terminal phase), allows it to prosecute targets at extreme BVR and places it among the longest-range air-to-air missiles currently in service globally. The dual-pulse motor significantly increases the missile's average velocity across the entire flight envelope, boosting the no-escape zone (NEZ). The missile's key feature is its miniature AESA seeker. The AESA seeker provides superior angle-off capability, greater resistance to jamming and better performance against stealthy targets, significantly increasing the probability of a kill compared to older active radar homing (ARH) missiles.

AIM-120 AMRAAM C-5/C-7

The AIM-120 AMRAAM (Advanced Medium-Range Air-to-Air Missile)[49] is a US-designed active radar-guided missile employed by the PAF's F-16 fleet. Its primary operational feature is its 'active radar homing' capability in the terminal phase, which is preceded by mid-course inertial guidance potentially updated via a data-link from the launching F-16. The launch aircraft can immediately turn away after firing – the essence of the 'fire-and-forget' concept. The versions operated by the PAF, typically the C-5 or C-7 variants, feature enhanced electronic counter-countermeasures (ECCM) processing and higher-G manoeuvring capability via cropped fins, providing a highly reliable, high-G-capable missile with excellent performance in a jammed electronic environment.

Face-offs: Comparing Key Aircraft and Missile Systems Used by India and Pakistan

Face-off: Comparing the AMRAAM, PL-15 and Meteor air-to-air missiles

The evolution of BVR air-to-air combat is best encapsulated by a comparison of three formidable missiles: the American AIM-120 AMRAAM, the European MBDA Meteor and the Chinese PL-15. While all share the foundational goal of striking an enemy aircraft before it is even seen, their design philosophies, and consequently their lethality profiles, diverge significantly, reflecting a generational shift in air combat technology.

The AMRAAM, particularly in its latest AIM-120D incarnation, serves as the established benchmark. A triumph of late-twentieth and early-twenty-first-century engineering, its greatest strength lies in its maturity, proven combat record and unmatched interoperability, seamlessly integrating with virtually every major Western fighter platform, from legacy F-16s to cutting-edge F-35s. Powered by a traditional solid-propellant rocket motor, the AMRAAM boasts a range above 100 km (in the D variant) and a sophisticated guidance package, including GPS-aided inertial navigation and a two-way datalink for mid-course updates. It is the reliable workhorse of the sky, but its propulsion system, which delivers a potent but relatively short burst of acceleration, means its energy quickly bleeds away as it travels its furthest reaches, limiting the size of its all-important 'no escape zone' (NEZ).

Stepping decisively beyond this traditional model is the MBDA Meteor. Conceived specifically to overcome the kinematic limitations of solid-fuel missiles, the Meteor incorporates a revolutionary ramjet engine. This throttleable ducted rocket allows the missile to 'breathe' air and sustain continuous, controlled propulsion long after a solid-rocket motor would have burned out.

The result is a dramatic increase in average velocity and kinetic energy throughout its flight path, particularly in the terminal phase. This sustained power translates into an NEZ rumoured to be several times larger than that of the AMRAAM, making evasion an extraordinarily difficult proposition for even the most agile targets at extreme ranges. The Meteor is the kinetic energy king, prioritising endgame speed and manoeuvrability above all else to ensure a near-certain kill.

Finally, the PL-15 represents China's latest leap into the realm of modern BVR air warfare. While specific details remain closely guarded, the PL-15 is widely believed to be propelled by a dual-pulse solid rocket motor, which allows for a secondary ignition to provide sustained thrust during the mid-course or terminal phase. It is believed that the variant has a range of 250 km. This design choice grants it a significantly extended range, exceeding the range of the AIM-120D. Moreover, the PL-15 is distinguished by its compact, cropped fins, designed to facilitate internal carriage within Chinese stealth aircraft such as the J-20, and by its purported integration of an AESA radar seeker. This AESA seeker, a major technological advance, offers superior ECCM and precision, marking the PL-15 as a strategic threat not only to frontline fighters but also to high-value support assets like AWACS and refuelling tankers, which it is designed to neutralise from vast distances.

In essence, the AMRAAM is the globally deployed, combat-proven standard, known for its versatility; the Meteor is the technological pacesetter, dominating the kinematic fight with its game-changing ramjet;

and the PL-15 is the formidable new challenger, combining a dual-pulse motor with advanced AESA guidance to achieve exceptional reach and stealth carriage compatibility. They are three distinct expressions of the modern imperative: to hit faster, fly farther and leave the enemy with nowhere to run.

Face-off: CM-400 vs BrahMos-A

The realm of air-launched anti-ship and land-attack weapons has been profoundly reshaped by the drive for speed, placing the air-launched BrahMos-A and the Chinese CM-400AKG (often simply referred to as CM-400) in direct, if asymmetrical, comparison. Both missiles represent a high-supersonic, standoff strike capability, yet they achieve their lethality through fundamentally different design philosophies, reflecting a contrast between a ramjet-powered cruise missile and a solid-fuelled quasi-ballistic weapon.

The BrahMos-A, the air-launched variant of the famous Indo-Russian missile, is the epitome of a heavy, high-speed cruise missile. It utilises a two-stage propulsion system: a solid booster to achieve supersonic speed, followed by a liquid ramjet engine that sustains its blistering speed of around Mach 2.8

throughout its cruise phase. This sustained velocity and a large, heavy airframe (around 2.5 tonnes for the air-launched version) translates into immense kinetic energy on impact, granting it unparalleled destructive power against large naval vessels or hardened targets.

Its flight profile is generally characterised by a cruise phase, followed by a sea-skimming trajectory as low as 5–10 m above the waves in its terminal attack, making it exceptionally difficult for modern ship-borne air defences to engage before impact. The BrahMos-A is a long-range strategic weapon, with the standard version reaching between 290 and 450 km, prioritising a devastating, sustained supersonic strike from a substantial standoff distance.

In contrast, the CM-400AKG presents a smaller, lighter and more tactically flexible weapon. It is widely considered a derivative of a short-range ballistic missile system and is powered by a solid-fuel rocket motor, sometimes featuring a dual-pulse capability. Its great distinction lies in its flight trajectory: instead of maintaining a low cruise, it adopts a semi-ballistic profile, launching from a high altitude, accelerating to speeds potentially approaching or exceeding Mach 5 and then performing a high-angle, steep terminal dive. This approach grants the missile two key advantages:

speed at the point of impact, and a highly challenging interception profile for traditional surface-to-air missile systems, which are typically optimised for cruise missiles or aircraft, not high-speed, steep-diving objects. However, its propulsion system and flight profile generally limit its range to a shorter envelope, typically cited to be 100–240 km.

In essence, the air-launched BrahMos-A is the strategic heavyweight, a long-range, ramjet-sustained projectile designed for maximum kinetic devastation and a proven sea-skimming capability. The CM-400AKG is the tactical speedster, a lighter, high-Mach projectile that leverages a quasi-ballistic profile and sheer terminal speed to overwhelm point defences, operating effectively within a shorter-range engagement envelope. They represent two equally dangerous, high-supersonic solutions to the problem of penetrating modern air and missile defences, each bringing a unique blend of range, speed and attack geometry to the battlefield.

Face-off: S-400 vs HQ-9

The comparison between the Russian S-400 Triumf and the Chinese HQ-9 (HongQi-9) is a study in advanced long-range air defence systems, with the former representing a pinnacle of indigenous Russian engineering evolution and the latter being a highly capable, yet derivative, hybrid design. Both systems are the crucial shields of their respective nations, designed to enforce anti-access/area-denial (A2/AD) envelopes by intercepting a wide spectrum of aerial threats, from high-flying aircraft and cruise missiles to short- and medium-range ballistic missiles.

The HQ-9 is a testament to China's rapid advancement, having been heavily influenced by early variants of the Russian S-300 and incorporating technologies reminiscent of the American Patriot system. It is a capable, medium- to long-range system, with its latest HQ-9B variant extending its reach against aerodynamic targets to a significant 250–300 km. Its engagement radar, the HT-233 phased array, provides robust tracking, and its missiles utilise a combination of inertial, command and terminal active radar guidance. The HQ-9 is designed for maximum mobility, offering a rapid deployment time for its TELs. In the context of the region, the HQ-9 offers a significant, multi-layered air defence capability, designed to hold the line against fourth-generation fighters and standoff weapons.

However, the S-400 Triumf stands as the more formidable and technologically advanced of the two, representing a clear generational leap beyond the design lineage that influenced the HQ-9. Its defining feature is its layered missile capability, allowing a single battery to employ a range of missiles to engage threats at different ranges and altitudes simultaneously. Most notably, the S-400 can deploy missiles, which extends its reach against aircraft to a staggering 400 km, providing a deep strategic shield unparalleled by the HQ-9. Furthermore, the S-400's sophisticated multi-band radar suite, including the 91N6E Big Bird acquisition radar, offers a significantly greater detection and tracking range, reportedly up to 600 km, and can manage a vastly higher number of targets and guided missiles concurrently.

Where the S-400 truly excels is in its speed and anti-ballistic capability. Its interceptors, capable of reaching speeds up to Mach 14, are designed to counter extremely high-speed threats, and its anti-ballistic missile (ABM) capacity is proven and more robust than that of the HQ-9. This allows it to address tactical ballistic missiles with higher probability of kill. The system also integrates more advanced ECCM and specialised anti-stealth detection modes, making it a greater threat to fifth-generation aircraft.

In summary, while the HQ-9 is a highly effective, modern air defence system that provides a wide and reliable area defense, the S-400 is the undisputed strategic superior. It offers a deeper defensive envelope, a more versatile missile family, greater radar and tracking capacity and a superior defence against the most advanced, high-speed ballistic threats, making it the more potent and comprehensive long-range surface-to-air platform available today.

IAF Gallantry Award Citations[50]

Group Captain Ranjeet Singh Sidhu, Flying (Pilot)

During an operation, his squadron equipped with the formidable fighter aircraft, was chosen for strike missions over a predetermined target. His squadron subsequently conducted successful strikes over the targets and achieved the desired objectives.

As the Commanding Officer, Group Captain Ranjeet Singh Sidhu exhibited exceptional acts of gallantry on multiple occasions, displayed resolute leadership and unwavering dedication to duty in a complex and high-stakes combat environment with disregard to personal safety. He ensured the planning and execution of air operations of his squadron from three different locations along the Western sector. He led from the front by flying multiple deep-penetration strike missions to destroy the designated targets with surgical precision and flew Air Defence missions in aid of own forces flying similar strike missions. In each of these missions, he faced complex threat scenarios and layered air defences. Despite overwhelming odds, he demonstrated unmatched courage and outstanding tactical acumen, thus ensuring mission success. His constant liaison and advise to war planning staff ensured achievement of all mission objectives. Group Captain Ranjeet Singh Sidhu made dynamic, real-time decisions in the air, adapting swiftly to emerging threats and operational variables. His bold leadership and composure under fire were instrumental in achieving the intended strike outcomes while ensuring survivability of own forces that were undertaking missions under the AD cover of his squadron.

Beyond his own missions, he remained deeply engaged in inspiring, motivating and professionally guiding the squadron personnel. As the Commanding Officer of the unit, he executed the preparatory tasks and undertook operations with outstanding leadership. He motivated all the officers and airmen placed under his command to keep the aircraft combat ready and serviceable over extended periods during the operations. The IAF was able to achieve an enhanced offensive posture owing to the unequivocal results achieved by the sqn under his leadership. For his act of exceptional gallantry and courage, Group Captain Ranjeet Singh Sidhu is awarded 'VIR CHAKRA'.

Group Captain Manish Arora, SC, Flying (Pilot)

During an operation, he flew as mission leader of an unescorted strike package to neutralise predetermined targets that were heavily fortified by advanced weapon system of opposing forces. The airspace had seamless radar cover and was defended round the clock by aircraft equipped with long range state of art beyond visual range missiles. Opportunity to penetrate this hostile threat envelope was limited and launch window to deliver the weapon was significantly short. His profile entailed tactical formation routing at low level by dark night followed by aggressive manoeuvring, so as to achieve launch parameters to deliver the weapon accurately and simultaneously evade hostile defences.

Despite overwhelming presence of the opposing forces in large numbers, he fired his weapon on the designated targets keeping mission objectives above personal safety. During weapon delivery, he was flying under adversary's lethal ranges and had multiple aerial and ground launches on him. He not only ensured successful target destruction, but alerted his formation ensuring safety of his wingmen. During the operation, his audacious and aggressive manoeuvring plunged the opposing forces into tactical chaos. The attacks carried out by him and his unit against the adversary were so intense that they rendered them incapable of retaliating. He maintained composure and mission focus, enabling the strike team to achieve its objective with nil attrition. As Commanding Officer of the squadron, he upheld the motivation and morale of all personnel in his unit during the operation.

His dynamic leadership, expertise in battlefield management and courage inspired confidence not only in other pilots of his unit but in all air warriors. For his act of exceptional gallantry and courage, Group Captain Manish Arora, Shaurya Chakra, is awarded 'VIR CHAKRA'.

Group Captain Animesh Patni, Flying (Pilot)

During an operation, the officer was stationed at a forward airbase, commanding a strategic Surface to Air Missile (SAM) squadron. On the designated day, he demonstrated exceptional leadership, guiding his team with precision and flair, resulting in a decisive blow to the capabilities of adversaries, inflicting significant losses without suffering any damage.

The officer's contributions during the operation were instrumental, as he supervised surveillance over a very largearea and controlled two firing units. His unwavering focus, unrelenting drive and ability to devise innovative solutions to complex problems ensured substantial losses of opposing forces while safeguarding his equipment, even in the face of intense fire. During the Ops, as Commanding Officer, his unit engaged multiple aerial targets. The Unit dynamically relocated to deceive the adversaries and continued to maintain offensive posture. The destruction achieved by his unit thwarted strike missions of opposing forces.

Group Captain Animesh Patni's foresight, meticulous planning, and liaison skills were evident in the successful conduct of a pioneering Offensive Air Defence Operation. Moreover, under his watchful eye and robust security setup, the squadron apprehended a suspected enemy Intelligence Operative near their operational location. The officer's exemplary leadership, discipline, and management skills ensured incident-free and effective firepower throughout the operation. The high morale and positivity within the squadron are a testament to his ability to motivate and inspire personnel under his command. For his act of exceptional gallantry and courage, Group Captain Animesh Patni is awarded 'VIR CHAKRA'.

Group Captain Kunal Kalra, Flying (Pilot)

During tasking of an operation on short notice, officer ensured all his aircrew and aircraft were mission ready. On a designated day, he flew as mission leader of an unescorted strike package to neutralise predetermined targets that were heavily fortified by modern air defence weapon system. Opportunity to penetrate this hostile threat envelope was limited and launch window to deliver the weapon was miniscule. He was tasked to destroy two targets while navigating through adverse weather en-route. His profile entailed tactical formation routing at low level by dark night followed by aggressive manoeuvring to achieve launch parameters so as to deliver the weapon accurately.

Despite encountering aircraft unserviceability in air and overwhelming presence of adversaries in large numbers, he fired his first weapon on the target keeping Mission Objectives over his personal safety. First objective was achieved and he proceeded towards his second target. While readying his weapon for firing, system displayed indication of malfunction. Officer undauntingly kept flying under lethal range of opposing forces, evaded multiple aerial and ground launches. He executed remedial actions to reset his weapon system and brought his weapon back online. He not only ensured successful second target destruction, but also ensured safety of his wingmen. The stakes of the mission were extremely high and he proved his leadership and mission commitment. He dynamically re-allotted one remaining target in air to another formation ensuring complete target annihilation. As Flight Commander of the squadron, he upheld the morale of all the personnel in his unit during the operation, while supervising mission planning and asset management, ensuring unit readiness for mission execution. For his act of exceptional gallantry and courage, Group Captain Kunal Kalra is awarded 'VIR CHAKRA'.

Wing Commander Joy Chandra, Flying (Pilot)

During an operation, the officer was tasked with executing a precision strike on predetermined targets. The operation required intricate planning, precise coordination, exceptional airmanship and highest level of situation awareness owing to presence of heavily networked Air Defence grid of adversaries, comprising of Air Defence ac and Surface to Air Guided Weapons (SAGWSs) equipped with modern long range missiles.

The formation flew at low levels on the tactical route to avoid detection by radars and at opportune moment pulled up to higher levels for weapon release. As the mission progressed, the strike package was challenged by rapid air response both by way of Air Defence aircraft and SAGWs. Despite a networked hostile threat environment in air and ground, the officer displayed exceptional courage, enhanced situational awareness and optimal decision making in hostile environment and ensured successful delivery of weapon and its successful guidance till impact on target. Throughout the mission, despite being within lethal range of weapon systems, he maintained calm and focus to ensure destruction of the designated targets. For his act of exceptional gallantry and courage, Wing Commander Joy Chandra is awarded 'VIR CHAKRA'.

Squadron Leader Sarthak Kumar, Flying (Pilot)

During an operation, as a part of the mission planning cell, Squadron Leader Sarthak Kumar played a pivotal role in the conceptualisation, coordination and execution of multiple deep strike missions. He methodically worked with steadfast commitment, unshakeable focus and in absolute secrecy. Employing his exceptional expertise in preparing the extremely high-value missions with minute precision, he ensured that every detail of the targeting plan was carefully accounted for. His methodical preparation of target folders and incorporation of precise intelligence data was instrumental in enabling mission success while mitigating operational risks.

Squadron Leader Sarthak Kumar played a pivotal role in two critical, high-stakes long-range stand-off strike missions. On the designated day, demonstrating unwavering composure and unrelenting tenacity under intense pressure, he successfully executed a deep strike mission targeting the assigned target with surgical precision. On the next day, Squadron Leader Sarthak Kumar was again tasked to fly a long range strike mission that resulted in the destruction of another critical target, thereby critically degrading the operational capabilities of adversaries and crippling its ability to wage war effectively. He executed this mission with unwavering commitment, despite countering the threats from multiple long range surface to air weapon systems and Beyond Visual Range missiles.

His actions, which were vital component of the strike element, directly impacted the capacity of opposite forces to resist, significantly contributing towards the achievement of all major operational objectives and ultimately securing a decisive victory. For his act of exceptional gallantry and courage, Squadron Leader Sarthak Kumar is awarded 'VIR CHAKRA'.

Squadron Leader Siddhant Singh, Flying (Pilot)

During an operation, three ac formation was tasked for Stand-Off precision strike on a predesignated target. This required precise engagement of particular structure with the weapon system that had limited stand-off capability and required precise control of weapon till impact. The operation entailed accurate planning, precise coordination, exceptional flying skills and highest level of airmanship owing to presence of heavily networked and integrated Air Defence, which included long and medium range Surface to Air Guided Weapons (SAGWs) and Air Defence aircraft armed with long range Beyond Visual Range Missiles.

On the early morning hours, as part of the precision strike package, the formation flew at low levels on the tactical route in order to avoid detection by radars and at opportune moment pulled up to higher levels for weapon release. As the mission progressed, the strike package was challenged by rapid air response both by way of Air Defence aircraft and SAGWs. Despite a networked hostile threat environment in air and ground, the officer displayed exceptional courage, enhanced situational awareness and optimal decision making in air and ensured successful delivery of weapon and its successful guidance till impact on target. Throughout the mission, despite being within lethal range of weapon systems, he maintained calm and focus to ensure destruction of the designated targets. For his act of exceptional gallantry and courage, Squadron Leader Siddhant Singh is awarded 'VIR CHAKRA'.

Squadron Leader Rizwan Malik, Flying (Pilot)

During a mission at midnight, he flew as deputy mission leader of an unescorted strike package to neutralise predesignated targets that were heavily fortified by latest and highly potent air defence weapon systems. Adversary's airspace had seamless radar cover and was defended round the clock by aircraft equipped with long range state-of-the-art beyond visual range missiles. The opportunity to penetrate this hostile threat envelope was extremely restricted and launch window available to deliver the weapon was miniscule. His profile entailed tactical formation routing at low level by dark night, aggressive manoeuvring to achieve launch parameters to deliver the weapon accurately and evade defences of opposite forces.

Despite overwhelming presence of the adversary, he fired his first weapon on the target keeping Mission Objectives over personal safety. During weapon delivery, he was under adversary's lethal ranges and had multiple aerial and ground launches on him. Even in such grave situation, he ensured successful target destruction, displaying dynamic decision-making. The officer carried out an additional attack on second target while flying in high risk engagement zone and successfully annihilated another target. In attack phase of flight, he was challenged by aggressive electronic countermeasures which were evaded successfully. During the operation, officer led multiple missions amidst escalated hostile flying environment and fired weapons on target rendering them inoperable.

He displayed resolute valour, tactically adapted audacious and aggressive manoeuvring to plunge the adversaries into tactical chaos. For his act of exceptional gallantry and courage, Squadron Leader Rizwan Malik is awarded 'VIR CHAKRA'.

Flight Lieutenant Aarshveer Singh Thakur, Flying (Pilot)

During an operation at midnight, he flew as part of an unescorted strike package to neutralise the predesignated target by executing precision weapon strike, which spearheaded military operations. The targets were heavily defended by potent Air Defence Weapon systems. The opportunity to penetrate this hostile threat envelope was limited and the launch window to deliver the weapon was miniscule. He also led a two aircraft unescorted strike mission on a crucial target on the same night.

Despite overwhelming presence of adversary, he courageously fired his weapon on the target amidst eminent threat showing disregard to his personal safety. He led his formation by routing at low levels at night while avoiding adverse weather, displaying exceptional situational awareness and courage.

During weapon delivery, his formation was under adversary's lethal ranges and had multiple aerial and ground launches on him. His formation achieved successful target destruction. During the operation, his audacious and aggressive manoeuvring plunged the adversaries into tactical chaos. His attack on adversary had devastating effect by rendering him incapable of retaliating. He maintained composure and mission focus, enabling the strike team to achieve its objective with no attrition.

Throughout the operations, he was actively involved in terrain and target analysis and mission planning. His commitment played vital role in overall mission success. For his act of exceptional gallantry and courage, Flight Lieutenant Aarshveer Singh Thakur is awarded 'VIR CHAKRA'.

Acknowledgements

This project would not have been possible without the active assistance of the Indian Air Force – Air Commodore Mohit Shishodia and his team handling media and public relations at Vayu Bhavan; Wing Commander Jaideep Singh, spokesperson, IAF; and Group Captain Indranil Nandi. Finally, this project would not have been possible without the blessings of Air Marshal Narmdeshwar Tiwari, Vice Chief of the Indian Air Force.

I am also indebted to Damien Symon, easily among the finest satellite imagery experts anywhere. Damien's technical inputs have proven exceedingly valuable to my work for several years – he has been a true guide and friend. I am awestruck by his ability to interpret data and imagery, changing the way geo-politics is reported.

Finally, I would like to thank my brilliant editor, Chiki Sarkar, for bringing together so many stories and accounts into one seamless storyline and for working with me constantly as we chased self-imposed deadlines to get this project done in fairly record time! It would not have been possible for me to do this without her superb skills as an editor.

I would also like to thank my copy-editor Krishna Sawant for working closely with me as we went through multiple iterations of the book with several changes through the journey of the edit.

Notes

1.   NDTV News Desk, 'Air Force Came Up With Pak Strike Plan Within 48 Hours Of Pahalgam Attack', NDTV, 2025, Operation Sindoor: Air Force Came Up With Pak Strike Plan Within 48 Hours Of Pahalgam Attack [accessed 23 December 2025].

2.   Press Bureau of India, 'Pakistan's bid to escalate negated – Proportionate response by India', Ministry of Defence, Government of India, 8 May 2025, https://www.pib.gov.in/PressReleasePage.aspx?PRID=2127670®=3&lang=2#:~:text=It%20has%20been%20reliably%20learnt,sectors%20in%20Jammu%20and%20Kashmir [accessed 23 December 2025].

3.   Site Admin, 'Pakistan Attempts Drone Infiltration at 36 Locations; India Retaliates with Precision Strikes', Newsonair, 10 May 2025, https://www.newsonair.gov.in/pakistan-attempts-drone-infiltration-at-36-locations-india-retaliates-with-precision-strikes/ [accessed 23 December 2025].

4.   Ibid.

5.   Shubhajit Roy, 'Intense shelling along LoC, Govt says Pak sent 400 Turkish drones to attack 36 locations', *Indian Express*, 10 May 2025, https://indianexpress.com/article/india/india-pak-tension-mea-briefing-operation-sindoor-9992963/ [accessed 23 December 2025].

6.   TOI News Desk, '"Armed drones launched at air defence sites in Pakistan, radar destroyed': MEA on India's retaliation', *Times of India*, 9 May 2025, https://timesofindia.indiatimes.

com/india/armed-drones-launched-at-air-defence-sites-in-pakistan-radar-destroyed-mea-on-indias-retaliation/articleshow/121033817.cms [accessed 23 December 2025].

7. 'Pakistani drones sighted at 26 locations along international border: Defence ministry', DD News, 10 May 2025, https://ddnews.gov.in/en/pakistani-drones-sighted-at-26-locations-along-international-border-defence-ministry/ [accessed 23 December 2025].

8. NDTV, 'Op Sindoor | "Very Easy To Start A War, But Not Easy To End It": Vice Chief Of Air Staff', Youtube, 2025, https://www.youtube.com/watch?v=Yeh1UR-jJ4w [accessed 23 December 2025].

9. HT News Desk, 'India-Pak ceasefire: What is Indian Army's DGMO post? Role explained', *Hindustan Times*, 11 May 2025, https://www.hindustantimes.com/india-news/indiapak-ceasefire-what-is-indian-armys-dgmo-post-role-explained-101746941073390.html [accessed 23 December 2025].

10. Press Information Bureau, 'Operation SINDOOR: India's Strategic Clarity and Calculated Force', Ministry of Information & Broadcasting, Government of India,14 May 2025, https://www.pib.gov.in/Pressreleaseshare.aspx?PRID=2128748 [accessed 12 December 2025].

11. Quwa Team, 'Chengdu J-10CE Dragon Multi-Role Fighter', Quwa, 18 March 2025, https://quwa.org/pakistan/air-force/combat-aircraft/chengdu-j-10ce-dragon-multi-role-fighter/ [accessed 23 December 2025].

12. 'PL-15 air-to-air missile', Army Recognition, 24 November 2025, https://www.armyrecognition.com/military-products/army/missiles/tactical-missiles/pl-15-air-to-air-missile [accessed 23 December 2025]; 'PL-15 air-to-air missile', Global Security, n.d., https://www.globalsecurity.org/military/world/china/pl-15.htm [accessed 23 December 2025].

13. Press Trust of India, 'Joe Biden will decide whether to apply or waive sanctions on India under CAATSA: US official on Russian S-400', *Economic Times*, 4 March 2022, https://m.

economictimes.com/news/defence/biden-will-decide-whether-to-apply-or-waive-sanctions-on-india-under-caatsa-us-official-on-russian-s-400/amp_articleshow/89963833.cms [accessed 23 December 2025].

14. Air Defense Vehicles, 'S-400 Triumf Triumph SA-21 Growler 5P85TE2', Army Recognition, 11 December 2025, https://www.armyrecognition.com/military-products/army/air-defense-systems/air-defense-vehicles/s-400-russia-uk [accessed 23 December 2025]; 'S-400 Triumf', Missile Threat, CSIS Missile Defense Project, 6 July 2021, https://missilethreat.csis.org/defsys/s-400-triumf [accessed 23 December 2025].

15. 'Transcript of Special Briefing on OPERATION SINDOOR', Ministry of External Affairs, Government of India, 8 May 2025, https://www.mea.gov.in/media-briefings.htm?dtl/39479/Transcript_of_Special_briefing_on_OPERATION_SINDOOR_May_08_2025 [accessed 12 December 2025]; India Today News Desk, 'Pak deliberately killed Sikhs, targeted gurdwara in J&K: India on LoC shelling', *India Today*, 2025, https://www.indiatoday.in/india/story/pak-deliberately-killed-sikhs-in-india-targeted-gurdwara-government-on-deaths-in-shelling-in-jks-poonch-2721713-2025-05-08 [accessed 23 December 2025].

16. Bilal Khan, 'Pakistan's C4ISR (Part 2): Land and Airborne Surveillance Systems', Quwa, 15 March 2016, https://quwa.org/weekly-report/pakistans-c4isr-part-2-land-airborne-surveillance-systems/ [accessed 23 November 2025]; 'AN/TPS-77 LONG-RANGE AIR SURVEILLANCE RADARS', Lockheed Martin, n.d., https://www.lockheedmartin.com/en-us/products/ground-based-air-surveillance-radars/tps-77.html [accessed 23 December 2025].

17. Quwa Team, 'Pakistan Army Inducts HQ-9/P Long-Range Surface-to-Air Missile System', Quwa, 17 October 2021, https://quwa.org/quwa-premium-excerpt/pakistan-army-inducts-hq-9-p-long-range-surface-to-air-missile-system-2/ [accessed 23 December 2025]; Analysis Defense and Security

Industry, 'Pakistan Leverages Its Alliance With China to Counter India's Air Power', Army Recognition, 29 April 2025, https://www.armyrecognition.com/focus-analysis-conflicts/army/analysis-defense-and-security-industry/pakistan-leverages-its-alliance-with-china-to-counter-indias-air-power [accessed 23 December 2025]; Pradip R. Sagar, 'Post-Operation Sindoor, why Pakistan's air defence hype stands crushed', *India Today*, 2025, https://www.indiatoday.in/india-today-insight/story/post-operation-sindoor-why-pakistans-air-defence-hype-stands-crushed-2791424-2025-09-22 [accessed 23 December 2025].

18. Aja Melville and Tom Freebairn, 'The Evolving Landscape of Loitering Munitions', Defense and Security Monitor, 28 February 2024, https://dsm.forecastinternational.com/2024/02/28/the-evolving-landscape-of-loitering-munitions/ [accessed 23 December 2025].

19. 'What Are Harop Drones? Weapon Used by India to Target Pakistan Air Defence Systems', *The Times of India* (2025), https://timesofindia.indiatimes.com/india/what-are-harop-drones-weapon-used-by-india-to-target-pakistan-air-defence-systems/articleshow/120995810.cms [accessed 5 January 2026].

20. Bilal Khan, 'Pakistan's HQ-16 surface-to-air missile plans', Quwa, 17 August 2016, https://quwa.org/daily-news/pakistans-hq-16-surface-air-missile-plans/ [accessed 23 November 2025].

21. https://en.wikipedia.org/wiki/CM-400; Bilal Khan, 'The JF-17's air-launched rocket (CM-400AKG)', Quwa, 3 October 2019, https://quwa.org/quwa-premium-sample/the-jf-17s-air-launched-rocket-option-cm-400akg/ [accessed 23 December 2025].

22. https://en.wikipedia.org/wiki/Akash_(missile).

23. Pallava Bagla, 'This Anti-drone system by DRDO is proving to be a nightmare for Pakistan', NDTV, 10 May 2025, https://www.ndtv.com/india-news/indias-home-built-d4-system-is-killing-pakistani-drones-all-about-it-8379576 [accessed 23

December 2025].

24. 'SPECTRA', Solutions Catalogue, Thales Group, n.d., https://www.thalesgroup.com/en/solutions-catalogue/defence/air/spectra [accessed 23 December 2025].

25. 'Statement by EAM Dr. S. Jaishankar on the Special Discussion in Lok Sabha on Operation Sindoor', Ministry of External Affairs, Government of India, 2025, https://www.mea.gov.in/Speeches-Statements.htm?dtl/39883/Statement_by_EAM_Dr_S_Jaishankar_on_the_special_discussion_in_Lok_Sabha_on_Operation_Sindoor [accessed 12 December 2025].

26. Sanstuti Nath, '"We'll Take Half World Down with Us": Pak Army Chief Asim Munir's Nuclear Threat in US', NDTV, 11 August 2025, https://www.ndtv.com/world-news/well-take-half-world-down-with-us-pakistan-army-chief-asim-munirs-nuclear-threat-in-us-9059544 [accessed 12 December 2025].

27. 'No Space for War in Nuclearised Environment, COAS Munir Cautions India', Dawn, 2025, https://www.dawn.com/news/1949711 [accessed 12 December 2025].

28. Sayan Ganguly, 'Vance Called 3-4 Times, I Was in Meeting: PM Recounts Op Sindoor Call with US Veep', *India Today*, 2025, https://www.indiatoday.in/india/story/jd-vance-called-3-4-times-i-was-in-meeting-pm-modi-recounts-op-sindoor-call-with-us-v-p-2763201-2025-07-29 [accessed 12 December 2025].

29. 'Statement by Foreign Secretary', Ministry of External Affairs, Government of India, 10 May 2025, https://www.mea.gov.in/press-releases.htm?dtl/39488/Statement_by_Foreign_Secretary_May_10_2025 [accessed 12 December 2025].

30. Abhishek Chakraborty, '"Pakistan Agrees to Immediate Ceasefire," Says Foreign Minister Ishaq Dar', NDTV, 2025, https://www.ndtv.com/world-news/pakistan-agrees-to-immediate-ceasefire-says-foreign-minister-ishaq-dar-8380472 [accessed 12 December 2025].

31. 'Foreign Secretary Vikram Misri during the Press Briefing on #OperationSindoor, Following the Ceasefire Violations', *Press*

Information Bureau – PIB, Government of India, 2022, https://www.facebook.com/pibindia/videos/645807878457374/ [accessed 12 December 2025].

32. Omar Abdullah, *X (Formerly Twitter)*, 2025, https://x.com/OmarAbdullah/status/1921224682159661251?lang=en [accessed 12 December 2025].

33. Stela Dey, 'India-Pakistan Agree to Full and Immediate Ceasefire, Announces Donald Trump', *The Indian Express*, 2025, https://indianexpress.com/article/india/india-pakistan-agree-to-full-and-immediate-ceasefire-announces-donald-trump-9994840/ [accessed 12 December 2025].

34. Narendra Modi, 'LIVE: PM Modi's Address to the Nation', YouTube, 2025, https://www.youtube.com/watch?v=bXxeQvuYP6o [accessed 15 May 2025].

35. Narendra Modi, 'PM Modi's Speech during Special Discussion on Operation Sindoor in Lok Sabha | English Subtitles', YouTube, 2025, https://www.youtube.com/watch?v=cn4UX_bD-4U [accessed 12 December 2025].

36. 'Breaking | IAF Chief Confirms 5 Pak Jets, 1 AW&c Shot Down by S-400 during Op Sindoor | Full Speech', *Www.youtube.com*, 2025, https://www.youtube.com/shorts/Tns1dXKm3_Y [accessed 12 December 2025].

37. Lara Seligman, 'Did India Shoot down a Pakistani Jet? U.S. Count Says No.', *Foreign Policy*, 2019, https://foreignpolicy.com/2019/04/04/did-india-shoot-down-a-pakistani-jet-u-s-count-says-no/ [accessed 12 December 2025].

38. https://en.wikipedia.org/wiki/S-400_missile_system.

39. 'Meteor', Air Dominance, MBDA, n.d., https://www.mbda-systems.com/products/air-dominance/meteor [accessed 23 December 2025].

40. https://en.wikipedia.org/wiki/Storm_Shadow.

41. R.K. Tyagi, 'Inside story: How Brahmos missile got integrated with Sukhoi-30 fighter plane', *ThePrint*, 29 November 2017, https://theprint.in/opinion/inside-story-how-brahmos-missile-got-integrated-with-sukhoi-30-fighter-plane/19329/ [accessed 23 December 2025].

42. 'Rampage', Air Surface Munitions, Elbit Systems, n.d., https://www.elbitsystems.com/air-space/air-surface-munitions/missiles-rockets/rampage [accessed 23 December 2025].

43. 'Popeye', Missiles of the World, Missile Threat, CSIS Missile Defense Project, n.d., https://missilethreat.csis.org/missile/popeye/ [accessed 23 December 2025].

44. Farhan Bokhari, 'Pakistan Unveils JF-17 PFX Fighter', *Janes*, 26 November 2024, https://www.janes.com/osint-insights/defence-news/air/pakistan-unveils-jf-17-pfx-fighter [accessed 6 January 2026].

45. Greg Waldron, 'China Continues Search for Fighter Export Success', *Flight Global*, 29 May 2025, https://www.flightglobal.com/fixed-wing/china-continues-search-for-fighter-export-success/163154.article [accessed 6 January 2026].

46. Wang Yanan, 'Pakistan Air Force Showcases Chinese-Equipped Strategy to Counter India's S-400 in Major Exercise', *China-Arms | Latest News and Reviews on Chinese Military, Army and Weapons*, 25 October 2023, https://www.china-arms.com/2023/10/pakistan-show-strategy-india-s400/ [accessed 6 January 2026].

47. 'ODIN - OE Data Integration Network', *Army.mil*, 10 October 2025, https://odin.tradoc.army.mil/WEG/Asset/HQ-9 [accessed 6 January 2026]

48. Douglas Barrie, 'China Fires Longer-Range AAM at Export Market', *IISS*, 8 October 2021, https://www.iiss.org/online-analysis/military-balance/2021/10/china-fires-longer-range-aam-at-export-market/, [accessed 6 January 2026].

49. 'AMRAAM Missile', Raytheon, RTX, n.d., https://www.rtx.com/raytheon/what-we-do/air/amraam-missile [accessed 23 December 2025].

50. 'The Gazette of India, October 4, 2025', Part 1 Sec. 1, Government of India, pp. 34–36, 4 October 2025 [accessed 19 December 2025].